WORLD
BOOK

The Secret Files
of Professor L. Otto Funn

Or Stop Being a Slug, Open This Book, and Make Your Brain Happy

World Book, Inc.
233 N. Michigan Avenue
Chicago, IL 60601
U.S.A.

For information about other World Book publications, visit our website at http://www.worldbook.com or call 1-800-WORLDBK (967-5325).

For information about sales to schools and libraries, call 1-800-975-3250 (United States); 1-800-837-5365 (Canada).

The Secret Files of Professor L. Otto Funn: Or Stop Being a Slug, Open This Book, and Make Your Brain Happy
ISBN: 978-0-7166-1324-4 (pbk.)

Printed in the United States of America
by RR Donnelley, Crawfordsville, IN
1st printing April 2013

TABLE OF CONTENTS

INTRODUCTION

DEAR READER:

Congratulations! You are now the proud owner of Professor L. Otto Funn's secret files, which will guide you through activities involving science, history, art, and more!

After Professor Funn mysteriously disappeared more than half a century ago, his files went missing. Decades later, the publishers of the *World Book Encyclopedia* discovered the files, along with Professor Funn's diary, in which he wrote instructions on how best to use the activities. The following is an excerpt from his diary.

June 16, 1947

At last, dear diary! After years of work, I have finally perfected the formula to impart the knowledge needed to embark on fantastic adventures! The key is to weave magic, monsters, mummies, and many more fascinating subjects into activities. What could be more fun than reading about sisters who have snakes for hair and can turn any man or woman into stone with their horrid glares? Or creating a compass to guide one's travels on land or at sea? A focus on science and engineering is required, too. And of course we must balance these pursuits with a foray into the arts, which helps to keep the mind's creativity at its peak.

I have created a list of guidelines for getting the most out of my secret files:

- Each activity involves a certain set of materials. One must gather these materials BEFORE embarking on any adventure, similar to how a cook must gather all the ingredients before baking a cake.
- Some of the activities may be completed within a few hours, and some require a day or longer. It is best to read through each activity before one starts to allow adequate time for its completion.
- Many activities require the assistance of an adult. Candles, knives, and blenders, for example, require years of experience and training to use safely.
- As a side project, I have developed blueprints for a mechanism I'm calling the *Internet*. I plan to include supporting materials for each activity on this "network" so that participants may access the materials from any location. Examples of such materials include videos, articles for further reading, and the occasional contest to inject a healthy dose of competition into one's endeavors.
- As a side project to the side project, I'm currently developing a set of quirky codes—*QR codes* for short—in the event that technology may one day catch up with my feverish brain. In the future, people may use these codes to link directly to the online materials using their mobile devices. (Yet another side project—I will write more on these devices in a separate entry).
- Finally, the secret ingredient required for each activity is FUN. When one is in a foul or sluggish mood, for example, it can sap the enjoyment from even the most engaging hours of play. In such cases, it helps to put on a disguise, such as a fake mustache, to free oneself of daily cares. I am working on a set of mustache designs that should suit any mood or occasion. I recommend that children use these mustaches while performing each activity or whenever they please.

I am long-winded today, dear diary, and I must now prepare for my own adventure in the Bermuda Triangle. I will write more once I arrive there.

Note to Reader: *This is the last entry of Professor L. Otto Funn's diary. He was never heard from again.*

CRAYON ROCK CYCLE

HAVE YOU EVER recycled an aluminum can? Our planet recycles its own materials in a similar way. For example, Earth recycles old rocks into new rocks. This process is called the rock cycle.

There are three main types of rock on Earth: sedimentary, metamorphic, and igneous (*IHG nee uhs*). The rock cycle describes how one type of rock changes into a different type. Weathering, erosion, pressure, and heat are the main forces that make the rocks transform. This process takes millions of years!

In this activity, you'll recreate the rock cycle using old crayons. To begin, pretend that each crayon is an igneous rock.

MATERIALS:

- Newspapers
- Pencil sharpener
- 4 old crayons, each a different color
- Aluminum foil
- Heavy book
- Muffin pan
- Foil baking cups
- Large bowl
- Ice cubes
- Warm water
- Oven mitt
- Camera (or art supplies) and writing materials

WEATHER *the crayons.*

In nature, a process called *weathering* breaks down big rocks into small pieces. Weathering is caused by wind, rain, and changes in temperature. On hot days, rocks expand. On cold days, rocks contract. These changes in temperature cause cracks to form. Eventually, the rocks break into pieces called *sediment.*

You will weather your crayons using a pencil sharpener. First, cover your workspace with newspapers. Sharpen one of the crayons over a piece of aluminum foil. Continue until you have a small pile of wax shavings. Now repeat the process with the other three crayons. You should have four separate piles of crayon "sediment."

Throughout the project, document the process with photography, video, drawing, graphing, writing, cartooning, music writing, or any other form.

Sedimentary Rock

The horizontal rock layers seen in these cliffs show layers of sediment that have piled on top of one another over time.

Layer the **SEDIMENT.**

Erosion happens when sediment moves from one place to another. Wind can blow sediment over great distances. Water currents can carry sediment out to sea. Layers form as the sediment settles.

You can make your own layers of crayon sediment. First, crease a large piece of foil in the middle. (The crease will make it easy to fold in half later.) Sprinkle one color of crayon sediment over one half of the foil. The layer should be about 1 centimeter deep. Repeat the process with the other colors. Now fold the foil in half to create a packet.

STEP 3

Make a **SEDIMENTARY CRAYON.**

Over time, many layers of sediment build up. The weight of the top layers creates a lot of pressure. The top layers press down on the bottom layers. Eventually, the bottom layers are smashed together into sedimentary rock.

To make a sedimentary crayon, place a heavy book over the foil packet. Press down on the book with your hands. Use as much force as you can. When you open the foil, the crayon sediment should be smashed together. Now you have a sedimentary crayon! Break off a small piece. Look at the layers. Take notes on what you see.

Make a **METAMORPHIC CRAYON.**

Metamorphic rock forms when heat and/or pressure cause a rock to change. This process takes place deep within Earth. First, a rock is buried deep underground. High temperatures or high pressure transform the old rock.

You will use pressure to make a metamorphic crayon. Arrange the pieces of your sedimentary crayon in a pile on the foil. Fold the foil to create another packet. Place the packet on the floor. Stand on it with all of your weight. Bounce up and down for a minute or two. When you open the foil, you will have a metamorphic crayon. Notice its texture, shape, and thickness. Break it into pieces and study the edges. Remember to take notes.

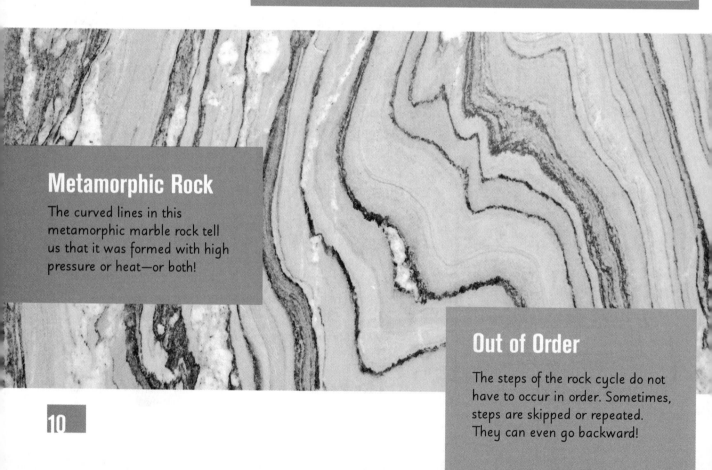

Metamorphic Rock

The curved lines in this metamorphic marble rock tell us that it was formed with high pressure or heat—or both!

Out of Order

The steps of the rock cycle do not have to occur in order. Sometimes, steps are skipped or repeated. They can even go backward!

STEP 5

Make an **IGNEOUS CRAYON.**

Igneous rock begins as magma. Magma is hot liquid rock that's under pressure. Some of the magma cools underground, where it turns into igneous rock. Some magma rises to Earth's surface in the form of lava. After a volcano erupts, the lava hardens into igneous rock.

Ask an adult to help with this part of the project. Preheat the oven to 250 degrees Fahrenheit. Place the foil baking cups in the pan. Place a fragment of your metamorphic crayon in each cup. Put the pan in the oven. Check it every 2 minutes. While you wait, put the ice cubes in the bowl. Add warm water. Remove the pan from the oven when all the wax has melted. (Don't forget to use oven mitts!) Carefully pour the melted wax into the ice water. Wait 2 minutes. Pull out the chunks of wax. These are igneous crayons. How are they different from the sedimentary or metamorphic crayons you started with? Take notes as you compare and contrast.

To watch a video

about the weathering process, visit: http://bit.ly/crayonrock

Igneous Rock

Granite is a common type of igneous rock. Most granite is formed by the slow cooling of magma beneath Earth's surface.

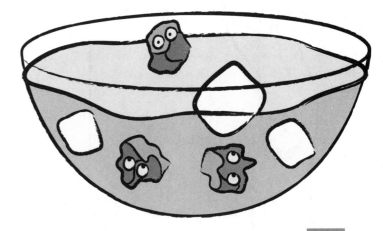

Hey — Stalagmite!

Hey — Stalactite!

GROW YOUR OWN STALACTITES AND STALAGMITES

UNDERGROUND CAVES contain all sorts of strange stuff. You might find bats, beetles, spiders, and other creepy critters. You might also see formations called *stalactites* and *stalagmites*.

Stalactites hang down from the ceiling. They look like icicles. Stalagmites rise up from the floors of caves.

While stalactites and stalagmites can take thousands of years to form in nature, yours will only need a few days.

MATERIALS:

- 2 glass jars (Make sure they're the same size.)
- Water
- Large bowl
- Measuring cup
- 1/4 cup Epsom salt (magnesium sulfate)
- Large spoon
- Food coloring (optional)
- Newspapers or a tray
- Yarn or thick string (Natural fibers like wool and cotton are best.)
- Scissors
- 2 metal washers or paperclips (or other small objects you can use as weights)
- Plate
- Ruler
- Camera (or art supplies) and writing materials

MAKE *the solution.*

Stalactites and stalagmites usually form in limestone caves. As water drips down from the ceiling and walls, it picks up a mineral from the limestone. This mineral is called *calcite*, and it forms a special solution with the water.

To make your own solution, begin by pouring hot tap water into each of the jars. (Leave an inch or two of space at the top.) Empty the jars into a big bowl. Stir in 1/4 cup of Epsom salt until it dissolves. Keep adding salt and stirring until the salt does not dissolve anymore. Add a few drops of food coloring, if you're using it. Now pour the salty solution back into the jars. Be careful not to spill!

Stunning Sights

Amazing formations and multicolored lights reflected in a pool create a stunning display in China's Reed Flute Cave. The cave is more than 180 million years old.

Throughout the project, document the process with photography, video, drawing, graphing, writing, cartooning, music writing, or any other form.

SET UP *your experiment.*

Most caves don't get a lot of visitors. Experienced cavers try not to touch stalactites and stalagmites. These formations are very fragile. They might break, change, or stop growing because of the natural oils on human hands.

To protect your project, find a place where it won't be in the way. (You shouldn't move it after the first day!) Spread out newspapers on a flat surface. Place a plate in the middle of your set-up. Arrange the jars on either side of the plate.

Cut a 24-inch (61-centimeter) piece of yarn and wet it with water. Tie a metal washer to one end of the yarn and drop it into one of the jars. Tie another metal washer to the other end and drop it into the other jar. The yarn should form a bridge that dips down between the two jars. The middle of the string should dip below the water level of both jars.

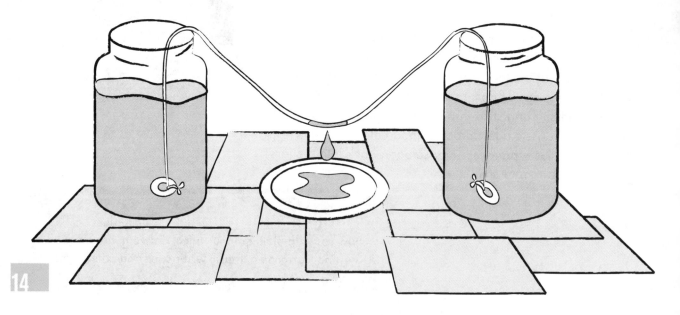

Watch what HAPPENS.

In caves, stalactites and stalagmites form when the calcite solution drips slowly to the ground. Over time, the water evaporates into the air, but the calcite is left behind. The calcite deposits build up, forming stalactites and stalagmites. This process takes thousands of years!

Luckily, your stalactites and stalagmites will form much more quickly. The salt solution will drip down from the middle of the yarn bridge. Soon, the water will evaporate. The salt that's left behind will build up on the yarn and on the plate.

Each day, watch for new growth. (Be patient—it might take a few days to see results.) Use a ruler to measure your stalactites and stalagmites. You can also measure the water levels in the jars. Record your findings every day for at least a week.

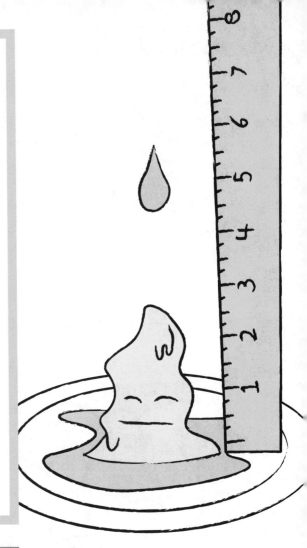

Which One's Which?

Having trouble remembering which way stalactites and stalagmites grow? Here's a neat memory trick: *Stalactite* is spelled with a C, which stands for *ceiling*. *Stalagmite* has a G, which stands for *ground*.

To learn more about caves, visit: http://bit.ly/growstalactite

EGG DROP

CAN YOU CONSTRUCT a container that will keep a raw egg from cracking when it drops from 5 feet? How about 10 feet? Or two stories? Give it a try!

MATERIALS:

- 6-12 raw eggs (You'll probably break a lot of eggs before you create your best design.)
- Measuring tape
- Notebook and pen or pencil
- Any materials you can find around the house or outside, such as: straws, pencils, rubber bands, recycled plastic bottles, string, fabric, plant matter, bubble wrap, grocery bags, cardboard, foam, tin foil, plastic wrap, paper towels, hand towels, rags, socks, plastic grass, packing materials, popped popcorn, aluminum drink cans, etc.
- Scissors
- Tape
- Newspapers
- Camera and/or video camera (optional)

THE RULES:

- You can't boil or otherwise tamper with the egg.
- You can't look up other people's designs on the Internet—that's cheating! Be creative. Use your imagination!
- You can't use a parachute for your carrier.
- Your carrier can't be longer than 18 inches (about 46 centimeters) on any side.

Experiment A: DESIGN YOUR OWN CARRIER

Before you get started, sit down and think about your design. Draw a picture of your design, and write down how each part of the carrier will work to keep your egg safe.

Collect your materials and start building your egg carrier. You can use any items you find around the house, such as bubble wrap, cardboard boxes, or socks. You may also use natural materials that you find outside. Record each step of the building process with a camera or video camera, or by writing in a journal.

Once you have built your carrier, test its design by placing your egg inside and dropping the carrier from a short distance off the ground. (Cover your work area with newspapers first.)

If your egg cracked, think about why your carrier did not protect the egg from the fall. How can you improve your design? Write down your thoughts and try again!

If your egg survived the first drop, test your carrier from a slightly greater height. Before each drop, have someone measure the height from your hand to the ground. Record the distance in your notebook.

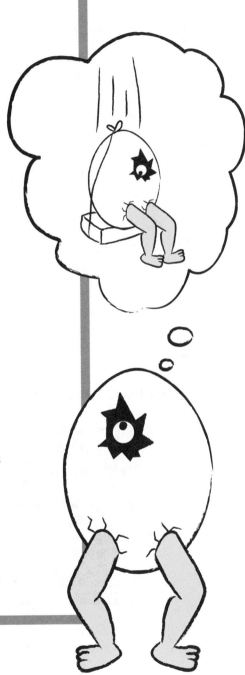

Warning! Raw eggs contain bacteria that can be harmful to people and pets. Perform this activity in an open space away from such items as food, carpeting, and furniture. Cover your work area with newspapers and be sure to clean up your area thoroughly. Wash your hands with soap and water after handling broken eggs.

Tips for Designing an **AWESOME EGG CARRIER**

If your carrier prevented your egg from cracking, congratulations! You are a #1 whiz kid. (Seriously. You should become an engineer at NASA. Don't know what an engineer is? Look it up!) But chances are, your egg did not survive a drop of more than a few feet. Want to know how to build a better egg carrier? Here are some tips.

A successful egg carrier design will:

- Ensure that the carrier drops vertically (straight down).
- Slow down the egg before impact, but not too quickly or the egg will break.
- Protect the egg by spreading the force of the impact evenly around the egg when the container hits the ground.

The following pages show three examples of effective egg carrier designs. You can try mixing and matching different elements from each design to create your own unique egg carrier!

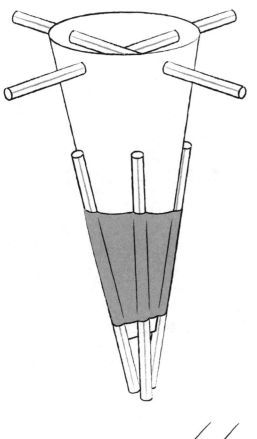

The **CONE**

This carrier is made of thin cardboard or poster board rolled into a cone shape. Four straws surround the cone and extend beyond the pointed end by an inch or so. The straws are then secured with duct tape.

The egg is surrounded by bubble wrap, which helps absorb the impact and prevents the egg from moving too much inside the cone. The two straws at the top of the cone form an X-shape that prevents the egg from falling out.

In this design, the straws around the cone absorb most of the impact as they spread apart and away from the egg. The cone shape also helps direct the force of the impact evenly around the egg.

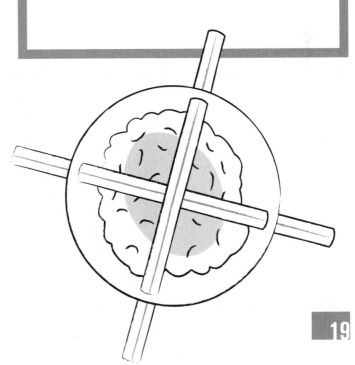

The CUBE

Use your school supplies to build a carrier that suspends your egg in mid-air! This design consists of two frames, each made of four pencils taped together. The frames are connected with four supporting pencils.

The egg is suspended in the middle of the carrier by four rubber band chains. Each chain is attached diagonally to opposite corners of the cube. The egg is wrapped in bubble wrap, which is then sealed with tape. The bubble wrap helps to protect the egg from the pressure of the rubber bands and secures the egg inside the web.

This carrier works best when dropped onto the bottom (the side that rests on four eraser ends) to help cushion the drop. The rubber bands help spread the force of the impact away from the egg. They also pull against each other, allowing the egg to move slightly in each direction.

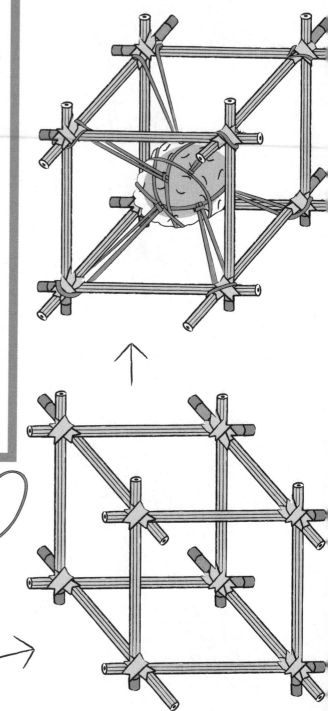

The Bottle ROCKET

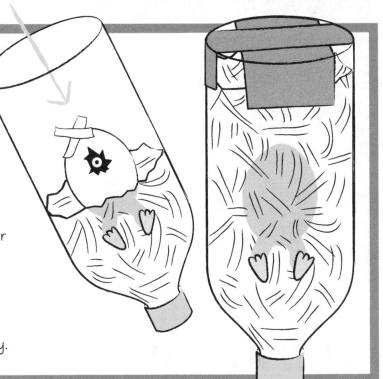

A liter-size plastic soda bottle can be converted into a rocket-shaped egg carrier! In this design, shredded paper surrounds the egg, allowing the egg to move without hitting the sides of the bottle. This limited movement helps to spread the force of the impact. The paper cushioning slows the egg down, but not so quickly that the egg breaks.

The cap of the bottle is filled with modeling clay, which adds weight to ensure that the carrier will drop vertically.

Experiment B: LET THE GAMES BEGIN

Now that you know how to build an awesome egg carrier, it's time to get serious! Create an egg drop competition with your friends. The winner is the person who designs a carrier that protects an egg from the highest drop. Get your video camera ready and get started!

You can add any number of rules to your competition. Here are some variations on the egg drop challenge:

- Limit each person to the same building materials.
- Start with a 5-foot (1.5-meter) drop, and then continue to increase the drop by 1 foot until all the eggs are broken!
- Use a timer to see which egg carrier drops the fastest while still protecting the egg.

Enter the World Book
Egg Drop Contest!

Submit a video of your egg carrier in action to World Book to enter a contest! Be sure to explain the design of your carrier and how each part helps to protect the egg. The person who designs the most original egg carrier (judged by World Book science editors) gets a prize!

For more information, visit:
http://bit.ly/eggdrops

MAKE YOUR OWN MUMMY

A MUMMY is a body that has been *preserved*, or kept from rotting. The most famous mummies are from ancient Egypt.

Ancient Egyptians believed in life after death. They believed that a person had the same body in the next world, so they wanted to keep the body in good condition.

At first, ancient Egyptians buried their dead in the sand of the nearby desert. The sand dried the bodies and preserved them naturally. Over time, ancient Egyptians developed a mummification process that took up to 70 days to complete.

In this activity, you'll follow the same steps as the ancient Egyptians to create your own mummy!

MATERIALS:

- Stuffed animal that can be taken apart (NOTE: DO NOT choose a treasured toy—or your brother or sister's favorite stuffed pal!)
- Linen cloth large enough to cover your stuffed animal
- Tweezers
- Shoebox or other cardboard box
- 4 small jars with lids
- Recyclable materials (for decoration): tinfoil, dried pasta, string, cardboard, beads, etc.
- Scissors
- Table salt
- Baking soda
- Cheesecloth
- Small, flat stones
- Old linens or newspaper
- Strips of white fabric, crepe paper, or toilet paper
- Drawing and/or painting supplies
- Dried spices
- Camera, video camera, and/or writing materials

STEP 1

Create a history FOR YOUR MUMMY.

Before you "mummify" your stuffed animal, give it a story! What was its name? Where did it live, and when? What was its job? How old was it when it died, and what was the cause of death?

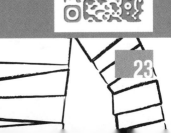

To learn more about ancient Egypt, visit: http://bit.ly/makeamummy

Remove THE ORGANS.

Ancient Egyptians removed all of the organs from the body, except the heart. They believed the heart contained the soul, which the person would need in the afterlife.

Ancient Egyptians removed the brain by pulling it through the left nostril with a special hooked instrument. Then they removed the stomach, liver, lungs, and intestines through a cut on the left side of the body.

Ask an adult to cut a hole on the stuffed animal's face to represent the nose. Use tweezers or another instrument to pull all of the stuffing out of the head through the nose.

Ask an adult to make a large cut on the left side of your stuffed animal's body. Remove most of the stuffing through the cut. Leave a little stuffing in the left chest area to represent the heart. Set aside the rest of the stuffing. (Don't throw it away—you'll use it in a later step!)

Tip: Ancient Egyptians made all of their incisions on the left side of the body. They believed the left side was holy because it is where the heart is located.

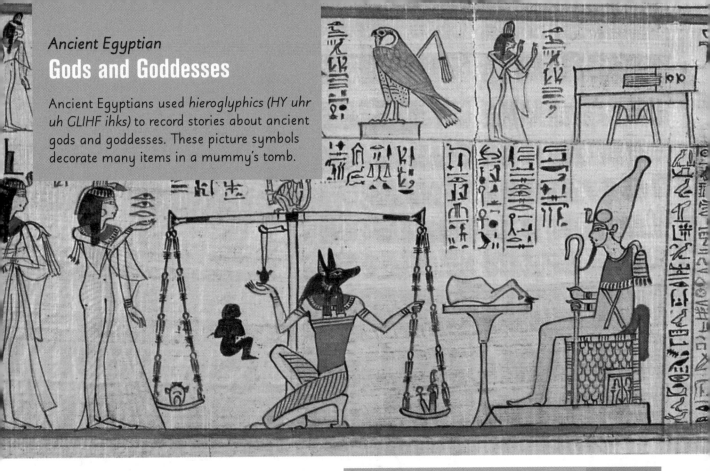

Ancient Egyptian
Gods and Goddesses

Ancient Egyptians used *hieroglyphics (HY uhr uh GLIHF ihks)* to record stories about ancient gods and goddesses. These picture symbols decorate many items in a mummy's tomb.

DECORATE JARS *for the organs.*

Ancient Egyptians placed the organs in containers called *canopic jars.* Use recyclable containers with lids for your mummy's organs. Decorate the jars with pictures of your stuffed animal. You can paint scenes directly onto the jars, or paint scenes on paper and then glue the paper onto the jars. When you are finished decorating the jars, place a small amount of stuffing in each jar to represent the organs.

Dry **THE BODY.**

Ancient Egyptians covered the body and organs with *natron*, a naturally occurring mixture of salt and baking soda. This substance drew moisture from body tissues, helping to preserve the body. Ancient Egyptians left the body to sit in this mixture for 40 days.

To "preserve" your stuffed animal, mix 1 cup each of baking soda and table salt. Pour this mixture over the stuffed animal and its organs.

CREATE CHARMS *for your mummy.*

Ancient Egyptians placed *amulets* (charms) in between the wrappings of the mummy. Some charms showed pictures or symbols of different gods and goddesses. Others were the Egyptian sign for life. The ancient Egyptians believed that these charms helped the person travel safely to the afterlife.

Paint pictures on the stones for your mummy. You can look up ancient Egyptian gods and goddesses, or create your own pictures and symbols.

WRAP *the body.*

After the body was dried, it was treated with substances that helped seal out moisture. The body could be stuffed with straw, linen, moss, or other material to give it a more lifelike appearance. It was then wrapped in linen bandages. Finally, the mummy was covered with a linen *shroud*, or cloth.

Fill the body of your stuffed animal with old linens or newspapers. To seal the body, wrap it in cheesecloth. Then take your strips of linen, crepe paper, or toilet paper and wrap your stuffed animal. As you wrap the body, place your amulets in between the wrappings. When you have completely wrapped the mummy, place a linen cloth over its body.

CREATE A MASK *for your mummy.*

Some Egyptian mummies had a mask placed over their head. Some masks resembled the face of the person so that their soul could recognize the body in the afterlife.

Cut the construction paper in the shape of your stuffed animal's head. This will represent its mask. Decorate your mask with a picture of your stuffed animal's face and place the mask over its head.

Gleaming Gold Mask

This lifelike gold mask covered the head and shoulders of ancient Egyptian King Tutankhamun's mummy.

Decorate **THE SARCOPHAGUS.**

Mummies were usually placed in a coffin called a *sarcophagus*. The coffins were made of wood or stone. The sarcophagus was often shaped like the mummy and decorated with religious pictures and *hieroglyphics* (picture writing). Egyptians also painted special symbols to protect the body or help the spirit on its journey to the afterlife.

Decorate your cardboard box, which will represent your mummy's sarcophagus. Include your mummy's name and any pictures you like.

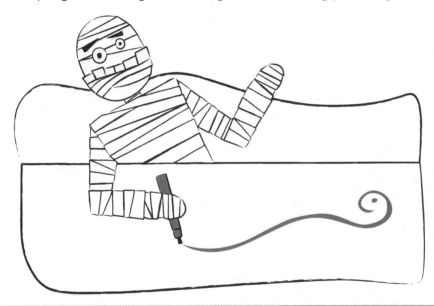

Throughout the project,

document the process with photography, video, drawing, graphing, writing, cartooning, music writing, or any other form.

STROCKET LAUNCH

ROCKETS HAVE MANY USES. Most of those uses involve serious lifting. Rockets are the only vehicles powerful enough to carry people into space. They are also used to launch big pieces of equipment like satellites and probes.

As a result, rockets are very heavy. The Saturn 5 rocket, which took astronauts to the moon, weighed more than 6 million pounds (2.7 million kilograms)!

In this activity, you will build a straw rocket, otherwise known as a "strocket." Even though a strocket weighs next to nothing, it demonstrates Newton's third law of motion—just like a real rocket!

MATERIALS:

- Large plastic straw
- Small plastic bendable straw
- Piece of paper
- Pencil
- Ruler
- Scissors
- Tape
- Modeling clay (or chewed bubble gum)
- Camera (or art supplies) and writing materials

Throughout the project, document the process with photography, video, drawing, graphing, writing, cartooning, music writing, or any other form.

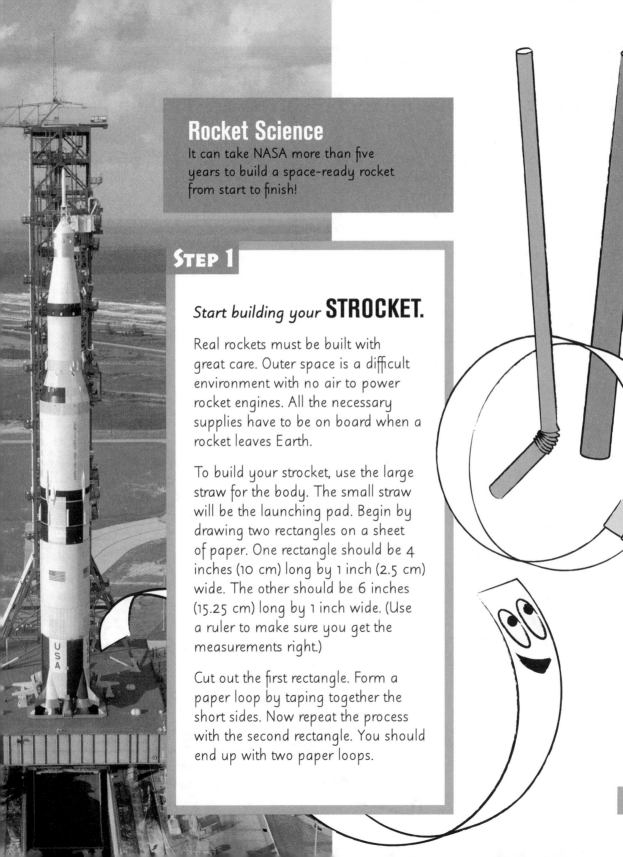

Rocket Science

It can take NASA more than five years to build a space-ready rocket from start to finish!

STEP 1

Start building your STROCKET.

Real rockets must be built with great care. Outer space is a difficult environment with no air to power rocket engines. All the necessary supplies have to be on board when a rocket leaves Earth.

To build your strocket, use the large straw for the body. The small straw will be the launching pad. Begin by drawing two rectangles on a sheet of paper. One rectangle should be 4 inches (10 cm) long by 1 inch (2.5 cm) wide. The other should be 6 inches (15.25 cm) long by 1 inch wide. (Use a ruler to make sure you get the measurements right.)

Cut out the first rectangle. Form a paper loop by taping together the short sides. Now repeat the process with the second rectangle. You should end up with two paper loops.

ASSEMBLE *the navigation system.*

It's easy to get lost in space! A real rocket uses a computerized navigation system to stay on track. Your strocket will use paper loops. Place the large straw through the small loop. Tape the loop in place about 1 inch (2.5 centimeters) from the end of the straw. Place the other end of the large straw through the large loop. Tape the loop in place about 1 inch from that end of the straw. Now your strocket should glide on a smooth path.

Prepare to **LAUNCH**.

Prepare to launch by inserting the small straw into the large straw. Make sure the bendy part of the small straw is at the same end as the large paper loop. Seal the other end of the strocket with a small piece of clay.

Did you know?

Rockets are especially valuable for military use, atmospheric research, launching satellites and probes, and space travel.

BLAST *off!*

Real rocket engines produce *thrust* by putting gas under pressure. The pressure forces the gas out of the end of the rocket. The gas escaping the rocket is called *exhaust*. As the exhaust escapes, it produces thrust. The thrust makes the rocket launch into the air.

A rocket launch demonstrates Newton's third law of motion, which states that for every action, there's an equal and opposite reaction. Your strocket demonstrates the same law.

To launch the strocket, place your lips around the launcher to form a seal. Now blow a big PUFF of air into the straw. Your strocket will blast off! (That's because your air can't escape from the plugged end of the straw. Instead, it will escape from the unplugged end, just like rocket exhaust.) Pay attention to how far the strocket goes and what path it takes.

Try it AGAIN.

Using the same steps, launch your strocket again. Does it go the same distance? Does it take the same path? Record your observations.

Now mix things up by changing your strocket in some way. Try removing one or both of the paper loops, or replace the clay with tape or another light material. Try repeating the experiment outside. How does the weather affect your results? Take notes as you go.

To learn more
about rockets, visit: http://bit.ly/strocketlaunch

LIQUID MARBLE

HAVE YOU EVER wondered why oil floats on top of water? It's because oil and water have different *densities*. Density is the amount of matter in a certain space. For example, a bowling ball is about the same size as a balloon, but the bowling ball weighs much more. It is denser than the balloon. It has more matter in the same amount of space.

In this experiment, you will create a "liquid marble" by combining liquids of different densities: oil, water, and rubbing alcohol.

MATERIALS:

- Newspaper
- Wide, clear glass
- Small, clear glass
- Masking tape
- Medicine dropper
- Household rubbing alcohol (isopropyl alcohol, 90 percent or higher)
- Vegetable oil
- Food coloring
- Camera, video camera, and/or writing materials

Pour the **LIQUIDS.**

Cover your workspace with newspaper. Pour water into the wide glass, filling it a little less than halfway. Mark the level of the water with a piece of tape. Then, tilt the glass until the water is nearly to the rim. *SLOWLY* pour about 2.5 ounces (75 milliliters) of rubbing alcohol into the glass. (The slower you go, the better this experiment will work!) The alcohol should form its own layer on top of the water. *SLOWLY* stand the glass upright, being careful not to swish the liquids inside the glass.

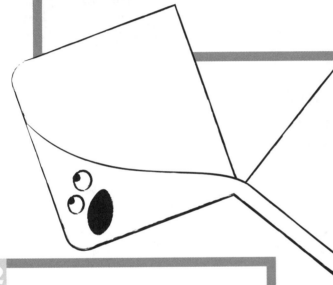

STEP 2

Add **COLOR.**

In a separate glass, pour a small amount of vegetable oil. Add a few drops of food coloring to the oil. This creates tiny swirls and drops of color in the oil, making it easier to see. The reason food coloring doesn't mix with the oil is—you guessed it— food coloring is mostly water. And oil and water don't mix!

Throughout the project, document the process with photography, video, drawing, graphing, writing, cartooning, music writing, or any other form.

When you pour oil into water, the oil breaks up into marble-sized beads. Eventually, the beads float to the top of the water and recombine to form a layer of oil.

Form a **LIQUID MARBLE.**

Using the medicine dropper, take up some of the colored oil. Put the tip of the dropper in the first glass between the water and the rubbing alcohol. Carefully squeeze the dropper to place the oil between the layers. Gently and slowly remove the medicine dropper. The oil should form a "liquid marble" between the alcohol and water. This happens because the oil is more dense than the alcohol, but less dense than the water.

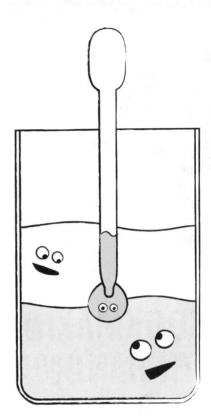

To watch a video

about this experiment, visit:
http://bit.ly/liquidmarb

REPEAT the experiment.

Temperature changes affect density. Materials—including water—expand when heated, making them less dense. When materials are cooled, the opposite happens, and materials get denser. Repeat the same experiment using materials with different temperatures. Try using cold water, cream, and oil. Or try using warm maple syrup, cream, food coloring, and oil. Observe and record how this experiment is different from your first one. How do these new materials change the liquid marble?

BOOKMAKING WITH HANDMADE PAPER

PAPERMAKING is an art that dates back to ancient times. In Egypt, people made paper by cutting thin strips from the papyrus (*puh PY ruhs*) plant. They crisscrossed the strips and pressed them together, creating a sheet of material they could write on. (The word *paper* comes from the word *papyrus*.) Today, most paper is made using wood that is processed into a pulp.

In this activity, you will first make your own paper. You can then bind your paper together to make your own book. You can fill your book with stories, photographs, pieces of art, or anything you choose!

To learn more about this activity, visit: http://bit.ly/makepaper

FIRST, *make your paper.*

STEP 1

SECURE *your paper mold.*

Ask an adult to staple the window screen or plastic mesh to the back or flat side of the wooden picture frame. This will serve as your paper mold.

MATERIALS:

- Old wooden picture frame, no larger than 8 x 10 inches (20 x 25 centimeters)
- Window screen or finely woven plastic mesh
- Stapler
- Stack of used white paper (printer sheets, old mail and envelopes, old telephone book pages, etc.) or any non-glossy paper
- Decorative materials, such as glitter, confetti, small leaves, flower petals, straw, or grass (optional)
- Food coloring or colored construction paper
- Blender
- Liquid starch
- Teaspoon
- Water
- Plastic tub, large enough to move the picture frame inside of it
- Stir stick
- Words, letters, and/or images from newspapers (optional)
- Old cotton tea towels or cotton sheets
- Sponge
- Horizontal drying rack, such as a cooling rack or oven rack

Create the PULP.

Tear the used paper into small pieces, no larger than 2 inches (5 centimeters) in size. These will serve as the base of the pulp. Fill a blender halfway full with the paper pieces. To color the paper, add several drops of food coloring or a use few handfuls of torn colored construction paper. Fill the blender with warm water. Let the mixture soak for about a minute to soften the paper. Ask an adult to turn on the blender. (Make sure the top is secure before doing so!) Blend until the mixture has a wet, mushy consistency, similar to oatmeal.

Make the **SLURRY.**

Fill the plastic tub halfway with water. Pour the paper pulp mixture into the tub. Stir the pulp into the water to create a slurry. At this point, you can add the organic materials and the decorative materials into the tub. Note: the amount of pulp you need to add to the water depends on the size of your frame and tub. For an 8-by-10-inch (20-by-25-centimeter) frame and large tub, add three batches of pulp. The more pulp you add, the thicker the paper will be. Lastly, add 2 teaspoons of liquid starch to the tub and stir, making sure that all the particles are suspended in the water.

Early papermakers created thousands of individual sheets of paper by hand. Each piece of paper was formed by placing a slurry mixture into a wooden mold to dry. It took workers many hours to make enough paper for a single book!

Transfer the slurry to YOUR MOLD.

Grasp the wooden frame on each side. With the screen side up, dip the frame into the back of the tub. Start with the frame in a vertical (up-and-down) position. Then slowly tilt the frame to a horizontal (flat) position until it is completely underneath the slurry. Gently move the frame back and forth through the water so that the slurry is evenly spread onto the screen.

Keep the frame horizontal as you slowly lift the it through the water. Hold the frame level above the tub for a minute or two to allow the water to drip off.

Helpful HINTS:

• If you did not get enough slurry on the screen, you can dip the screen into the slurry again. Or, if you have just a few bare spots, you can dip a ladle or large spoon into the slurry and carefully pour it over the thinner spots.

• Always stir the slurry before redipping.

• Remember to hold the frame horizontally to prevent the slurry from building up in one spot.

Separate the **PAPER**.

Lay a towel or sheet on a table top. Smooth out any wrinkles. The towel must be flat. Quickly flip the wooden frame onto the towel so that the screen side is flat against the towel. Your newly formed paper should be between the towel and the screen. Use a sponge to firmly and evenly press through the screen to release any water. (This step also binds together the paper fibers.) Do not rub! Instead, use a gentle blotting motion. Also, be careful not to move the wooden frame. As your sponge becomes soaked, squeeze out the water and continue to blot the paper.

When you cannot blot out any more water, carefully and slowly lift the wooden frame up, starting at the top edge and following through with one even motion to the bottom edge. If any small pieces are still stuck to the screen, you can carefully peel them off and press them into the paper on the towel.

Optional: You may want to cut out words, letters, and/or images from newspapers and stick them into the handmade paper before it dries. You can use these clippings to create a story for your book!

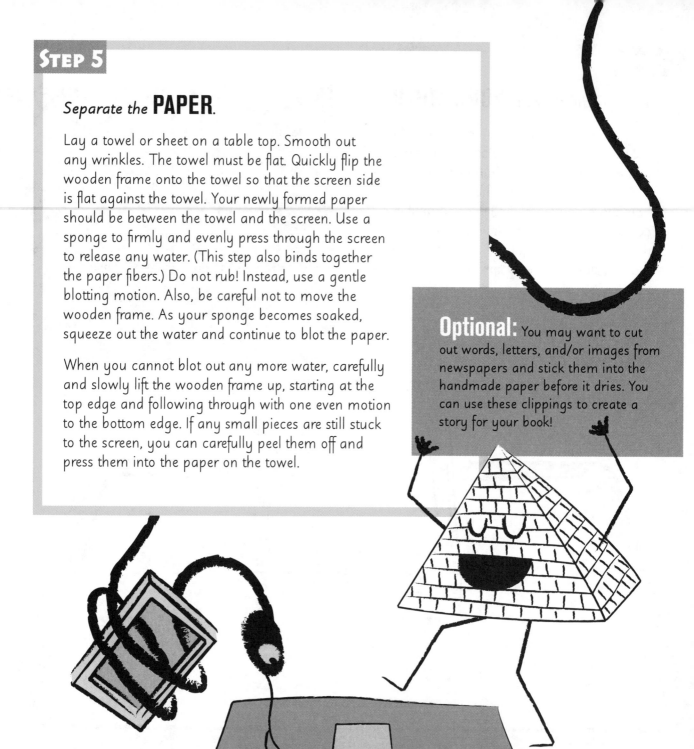

Handmade paper can be made with decorative items, such as flower petals or bits of seashells.

STEP 6

Let the paper DRY.

Let the paper dry partially on the towel. When the paper is dry enough to move, carefully transfer it from the towel to a drying rack. Let your paper sit for 24 hours.

Continue working through steps 1 through 6 until you have enough sheets of paper to fill your book.

Optional: If you do not like the uneven edges of your paper, you can use scissors to trim them.

Warning! Never pour the slurry down the sink because it can clog the pipes. When it's time to clean up, separate the paper pulp from the water by pouring it over the screened frame into another tub. Put the screened frame over your sink and pour the strained liquid through it. This second straining will ensure that little or no paper pulp goes down the drain. Remove the paper pulp from the screen, let it dry, and put it in the recycling bin. Save your wooden frame mold for the next time you make your own paper!

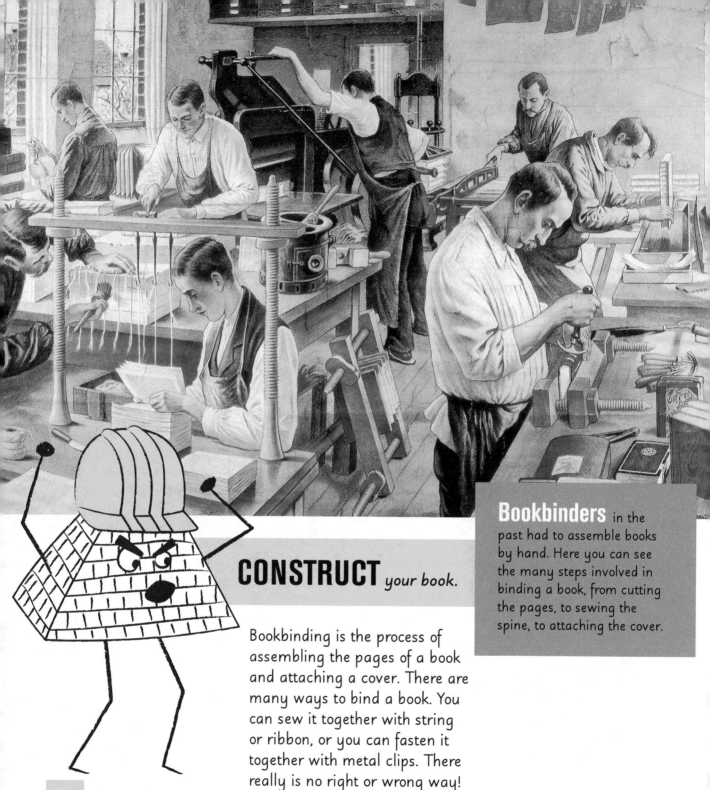

CONSTRUCT your book.

Bookbinding is the process of assembling the pages of a book and attaching a cover. There are many ways to bind a book. You can sew it together with string or ribbon, or you can fasten it together with metal clips. There really is no right or wrong way!

Bookbinders in the past had to assemble books by hand. Here you can see the many steps involved in binding a book, from cutting the pages, to sewing the spine, to attaching the cover.

MATERIALS:

- Many sheets of handmade paper (See instructions on pages 38-43.)
- Materials to add to the book (photographs, images, illustrations, pins, buttons, stamps, tickets, fabric, wallpaper, etc.)
- Glue
- Paper clips
- Heavy paper that can bend easily, such as bristol board
- Plain white paper
- Heavy string
- Hole punch
- Drawing/writing materials
- Camera, video camera (optional)

Create the **CONTENT.**

Decide what your book is about. Do you want to create a story or a piece of nonfiction about you or your family? You could draw a picture book, create a book of photographs, or include anything you choose!

After the paper is completely dry, add text and/or illustrations. If your paper is thick enough, you can write or draw on both sides of the paper. (Be sure to let one side dry before working on the other side.)

GATHER *the pages.*

Assemble the handmade pages in the order that you designed.

Take a sheet of plain paper that is slightly taller than your handmade paper and fold it into accordion pleats. The fold should be between 1/2 inch (1.25 centimeters) and 3/4 inch (1.9 centimeters) wide. The larger the paper, the wider the fold. The number of pleats you make should equal the number of pages in your book.

Start with your first handmade page. On the left-hand side of the page, place glue on both sides of the paper. Put the glue side of the paper into the first accordion pleat and press firmly. Using this process, glue each new page into the next accordion pleat. As you glue the pages, line them up so that the top of the pages are even. Allow the glue to dry completely.

Attach a COVER.

Cut a piece of heavy paper a little more than twice the width and slightly taller than the size of your handmade paper. Fold it in half. This will become your cover. Decorate both the front and back.

Place the pages inside your cover, making sure to line up the accordion pleat with the inside crease of the cover. Fasten paper clips to the top and bottom of your book. These will hold the pages and cover together while you sew the binding.

Ask an adult to punch an even number of holes into the folded side of your book cover and pages, about 1/2 inch (1.25 cm) away from the fold and about 1 inch (2.5 cm) in from the top and bottom of the book. You should have a minimum of four holes.

Tip: You can use any material that you can poke a hole through for your cover. For example, you can place the pages between a heavy fabric or even two pieces of cardboard.

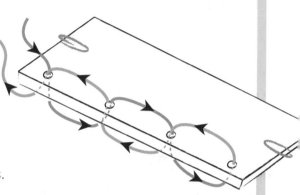

Optional: You can use different materials for sewing, such as wire, ribbon, zip cords, yarn, or even leather cords.

Beginning at the top of the book, thread the string through the holes. Be sure to leave some string at the top so that you can tie a knot. When you reach the last hole, begin stitching in the opposite direction. Look at the picture above for help. When you are finished, tie a knot to secure the stitches and then tie a bow. Enjoy reading your finished homemade book!

You CAN judge a book by its cover.

The cover is the first impression a reader has of your book. It should tell the reader what your book is about or reflect its content in some way. Spend time thinking about what type of design would best fit the content of your book. For example, if you are creating a book of poetry, you might want to paint an abstract picture on your cover. If your book is about an individual, you could glue a photograph of that person onto the cover. Have fun thinking up your cover design!

It is a wonderful day.

Handmade books come in a variety of formats. As you become more experienced at bookmaking, experiment with different designs for your books. You can play with the size, shape, binding, and material for each of your books.

生态银针茶饼

Throughout the project, document the process with photography, video, drawing, graphing, writing, cartooning, music writing, or any other form.

THE AMERICAN ARTIST Jackson Pollock (1912–1956) was famous for his "drip paintings," which consisted of webs of poured lines and drips. These unique paintings did not show objects, scenes, or people. Pollock was part of an artistic movement called Abstract Expressionism. This new style of painting influenced many other artists for years to come.

In this activity, you'll learn the same painting techniques used by Jackson Pollock to create your own masterpiece!

CREATE YOUR OWN MASTERPIECE

MATERIALS:

- Smock or old clothing
- Wood panel (medium-density fiberboard, multiplex, or regular wood), stretched canvas, or large sheet of white paperboard
- Primer (optional)
- Tarp or newspapers
- Nontoxic acrylic paints (Don't use oil-based paint. It will take longer to dry and is more toxic than acrylic paints.)
- Paint stir sticks
- Paintbrushes
- Writing materials and paper (optional)
- Camera or video camera (optional)

Prepare your workspace—AND YOURSELF!

Being an artist is a messy job, so be sure to wear a smock or old clothing so that you don't ruin your clothes. Also, ask an adult to help you choose a work area that's free of carpeting or furniture, such as a basement or garage. If it's a sunny day, you can work outside.

Cover your work area with a tarp or several layers of newspaper. It might be easiest to work on the floor. (Remember: if you clean up after yourself, you'll more likely get permission to do fun art projects in the future!) Place your wood panel, canvas, or paper in the center of the tarp or newspapers.

Students around the world visit local art museums to view artwork made by famous artists. This class is learning about one of Pollock's abstract drip paintings entitled *One: Number 31, 1950* at the Museum of Modern Art in New York City.

PRIME *the wood.*

If you are using a pressed wood product, ask an adult to *prime* the front and the back to prevent the panel from curving or bowing. A primer is a white coat of paint that protects and prepares a surface for further painting. Let the wood sit for about 4 hours, or until the wood is completely dry.

Let it DRIP!

To paint, Pollock laid his canvas on the floor. He worked from all four sides, dripping and splattering paint onto the canvas using brushes and sticks. Pollock also poured paint directly onto the work. Sometimes he stepped onto the canvas itself! Pollock painted until every inch of his artwork was covered.

Before you start painting, stir your paints. Then choose one color and drizzle the paint onto your board using the stir sticks or a paintbrush. Be sure to move around your work as you paint. Drizzle as much paint onto the surface as you like. Then select a new color and repeat the process until you feel your work of art is finished.

Jackson Pollock

DRYING *time.*

If you painted outside, wait a few hours before moving the painting to a safe place indoors. Let your painting dry for at least one day, or until it is completely dry. Once it is dry, ask an adult to hang your masterpiece in your room or in another area of your home!

Throughout the project,

document the process with photography, video, drawing, graphing, writing, cartooning, music writing, or any other form.

To learn more about abstract art, visit: http://bit.ly/makeamp

MAKE AND DISSECT YOUR OWN OWL PELLETS

Lemme' out!

OWLS ARE HUNTERS that eat a variety of other animals, such as mice, birds, reptiles, and fish. Like hawks, owls tear large prey into pieces when they eat them. But if prey is small enough, owls will swallow them whole. They later cough up pellets of bones, fur, scales, and feathers, which owls cannot digest. These pellets can be found under their nests and roosting places.

It's not a good idea to handle real owl pellets—or any other animal waste—because they carry germs. But in this activity, you'll create your own "pellet" to dissect. This activity works best with more than one person. Each of you can make your own owl pellet and then trade and dissect the other person's pellet!

MATERIALS:

- Brown felt
- Foraged materials: plastic bones, feathers, twigs, leaves, pebbles, plastic animals, etc.
- Large-eyed needle
- Thread
- Scissors
- Tweezers
- Pencil and notebook
- Camera or video camera (optional)

What Are Owl Pellets?

Owls have no teeth, so they cannot chew their food. Instead, they swallow their food whole or tear it into large chunks using their beak.

An owl's meal moves from the mouth into the *esophagus*, a tubelike organ. In owls, the esophagus leads to the *proventriculus*, a section of the stomach that produces digestive juices.

The food then passes into the *gizzard*, a section of the stomach that separates the nutritious content of the meal from the bits that can't be digested. Contracting muscles grind up the soft parts of the food, which then pass through the rest of the owl's digestive tract.

The gizzard then compresses the remaining indigestible material into a pellet. It pushes the pellet into the proventriculus, where the pellet is stored for hours. Before the owl can eat its next meal, it must *regurgitate* (throw up) the pellet. It does this by pushing the pellet up the esophagus and out through the mouth.

Owl pellets are an important record of the owl's hunting habits. *Ornithologists* (bird scientists) learn much about owls by studying their pellets. The bones, fur, feathers, claws, scales and other animal matter found in the pellet are evidence of the owl's activities. Often an entire animal skeleton can be found in an owl pellet!

Owl pellets are made of bones, fur, scales, feathers, and other materials that an owl cannot digest.

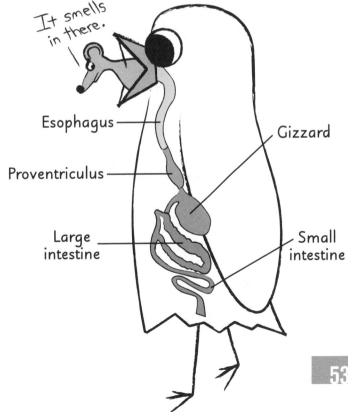

It smells in there.

Esophagus

Gizzard

Proventriculus

Large intestine

Small intestine

Where's my shoe?

STEP 1

Form the **PELLET.**

Cut a piece of felt roughly 3 inches (7.5 centimeters) square. Place the foraged materials in the center of the felt. Wrap the felt tightly around the materials to form the pellet. Sew the pellet closed so that the foraged materials don't fall out.

STEP 2

DISSECT *the pellet.*

Give the pellet to your friend. If your friend has also made a pellet, you can exchange them. Carefully cut open the felt with the scissors to reveal the contents of the pellet.

Remove each item with the tweezers. Catalog the contents of the pellet by drawing a picture of each item in your notebook.

Based on the contents of the pellet, write a story about the owl's life before it passed the pellet. What did it eat? Where does it live? Did it travel far from its nest? How old is the owl? Is it fat or thin?

To learn more about owls and hear some owl calls, visit: http://bit.ly/makepellets

STEP 3

Document your DISSECTION!

Document the pellet dissection through writing and photography or video. Discuss each object you found inside your pellet and what it tells you about the owl.

ART OF
NATURE

LAND ART is making art from something found in nature and assembling it in a natural environment. If you have ever built a sand castle on the beach, you have made a kind of land art.

A number of artists are known for their land art. In 1970, American artist Robert Smithson created a sculpture called the Spiral Jetty on the shore of the Great Salt Lake in Utah. The sculpture was made entirely of mud, salt crystals, rocks, and water. It forms a 1,500-foot- (460-meter-) long coil jutting from the shore of the lake. That's one large land sculpture!

You can become an artist and make your own land art! Create a structure out of branches or leaves, stones, grass, fruit, sea shells, sand, or anything you can find in nature. Let your creativity flow as you build your work of art!

MATERIALS:

- Items found in nature: twigs, sticks, branches, leaves, nuts and nutshells, flowers, grass, fruit, seeds, stones, sea shells, sand, etc. (Make sure that none of the plants are protected species!)
- Suitable outdoor space for the project
- Camera
- Picture frame (optional)

BUILD *your land art.*

Build or arrange piece of art outdoors using materials found in nature. For example, you can make a sun by using sticks and rocks, stones, and/or flowers. The sticks represent the sun's rays, and the rocks or flowers are the sun's *atmosphere* (the part of the sun that looks like a yellow circle).

Collect a variety of sticks and rocks. They can be tall or short, wide or thin, shiny or bumpy. Arrange the sticks in a wide circle on the ground. Leave some space in between the ends of the sticks in the center of the circle so that you can still see the ground. In this area, place the rocks in any formation you choose. Does your sun look like the land art in the photograph?

Sticks and Stones

Use your imagination to create unique land art, like this playful piece that looks like the sun. What other pieces of art could you make using sticks and stones?

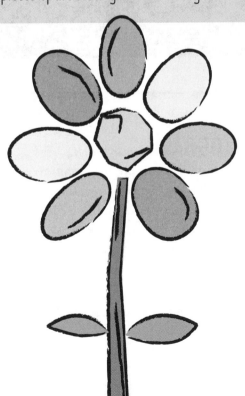

PHOTOGRAPH *your work.*

Observe and photograph your land art as it erodes, changes, or falls apart over time. If you use leaves or flowers, this might be a matter of a day. But if you are using such materials as wood or stones, it could take much longer.

Photography plays an important role in the work of some land artists. For example, British land artist Andy Goldsworthy often photographs his art during a natural cycle as it grows, changes, erodes, decays, or falls apart. The materials in Goldsworthy's art often include brightly colored flowers, icicles, leaves, mud, pine cones, snow, stone, twigs, and thorns. He often uses only his bare hands, teeth, and found tools to prepare and arrange the materials.

Icy Archway

Land artists create pieces of art from a wide variety of materials—even ones that can melt! In 1984, Andy Goldsworthy built the incredible arch seen here using hundreds of pieces of ice!

STEP 3

DISPLAY *your photos.* Frame your photographs to show how your artwork changed over time. You could also tack up your photos on a corkboard, display them on a collage, or use your images as screensavers on a computer or other digital device. (Be sure to ask an adult before using the computer!)

To see examples of different works of land art, visit: http://bit.ly/artofnature

MAKE A CARTOON FLIP BOOK

CARTOONS ARE MADE using a method called *animation*. Animation creates the illusion of motion instead of recording real action.

To make a cartoon the old-fashioned way (that is, without computers), a filmmaker photographs a series of drawings, one by one. Each drawing takes one frame of film. The position of a character or scene changes a little from frame to frame. When the film is fed through a projector, it appears to move.

You can create your own animation using only a pen and paper! In this activity, you will make a flip book, which is a group of drawings stacked on top of one another. In German, the word for flip book is *daumenkino*, which means "thumb cinema." A flip book is like a short animated movie—but it's on paper that you hold in your hand.

MATERIALS:

- Scrap paper
- Ruler
- Pencil
- Markers or pens
- 30 or more index cards
- Binder clip

PLAN *your story.*

Begin by choosing a topic for your flip book. Simple ideas are best because you need to make a LOT of drawings! The first part of your topic is a person, animal, or object—the star of your story. The second part of your topic will be the action, or what happens.

Once you have an idea, it's time to make a storyboard. A storyboard is a tool that writers and artists use to plan a cartoon. It looks like a giant comic strip. To make your storyboard, use the ruler to draw panels on the scrap paper. (Use a pencil so you can erase mistakes.) Then sketch out the action of your story. Keep in mind that your drawings should not be too complex. For example, draw a stick figure instead of a realistic person.

Idea Generator

Your flip book should be based on a simple idea that you can describe in just two words. Here are some topics you can try if you get stuck:

- Shooting star
- Bouncing ball
- Launching rocket
- Leaping fish
- Growing tree

ANIMATE *the story.*

Before computers were invented, a full-length animated movie could require tens of thousands of drawings. To animate your flip book, you need to use at least 30 index cards—maybe more. Begin by drawing the first index card and the last index card. Now draw all the cards that go in the middle. Each drawing should change only slightly from one card to the next. For example, to show a person kicking a ball, you might change the position of its legs and shift its position a little to the left or right in each drawing. Use a ruler to keep track of the position of the figure/object on each card. This way, your figure/object won't look like it's jumping back and forth—unless you want it to!

Tips: Draw only on the right-hand side of the card. (The left-hand side won't be visible when you flip.) As you work, flip through the cards to make sure the action looks right. When there's a big jump, insert an extra index card or two. When you're finished, the action should look smooth and continuous.

Bind your **BOOK.**

Bookbinding is the process of putting the pages of a book between covers. Use a new index card to make a front cover for your flip book. The front cover should tell readers about the story. Think of a title and write it at the top of the card. Then illustrate the cover. You can use one of the drawings from your flip book or draw something new. Make sure to leave room for the name of the author. (That's you!)

Use another index card for the back cover. The back cover usually gives readers information about both the story and the author. Since you don't have much room, just write one or two sentences about yourself. (You might include where you were born, how old you are, and your favorite hobbies.) When you have finished, arrange the index cards in order and place them between your covers. Secure the cards with a binder clip on the left side of the stack.

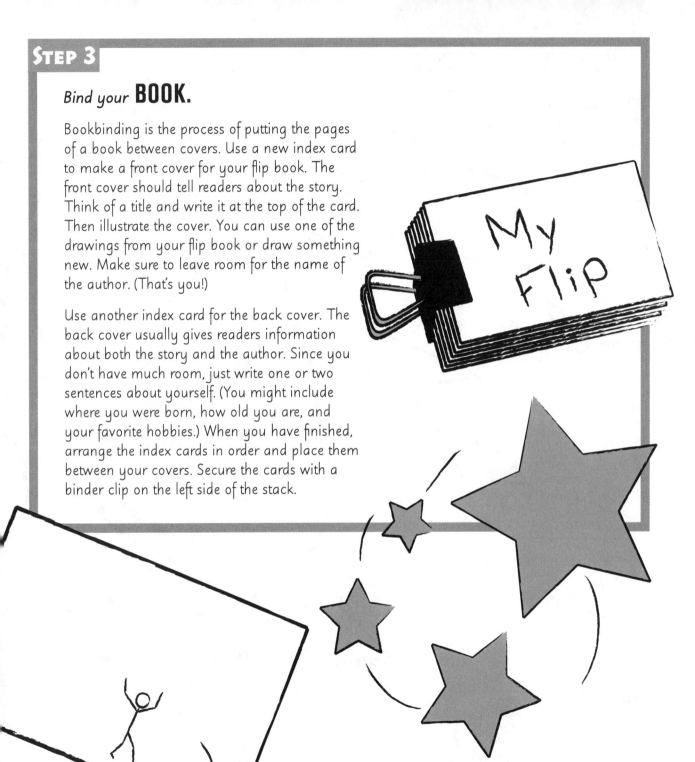

Windsor McCay was a pioneer of early animation. His most famous animated short film was *Gertie the Dinosaur* (1914), a story about a trained dinosaur.

To watch the animation, visit: http://bit.ly/cartoonflip

FLIP *it!*

When you see an image, your eye continues to see it for one-tenth of a second after it goes away. This phenomenon is called *persistence of vision*. Persistence of vision makes a series of still images—like your flip book drawings—look like they are in motion.

To watch your cartoon flip book, grip the clipped side of your book in one hand. Use the tips of your fingers on the other hand to flip through the pages. The speed of your cartoon depends on how fast you flip. Want to rewind? Try flipping through the pages back to front.

MAKE YOUR OWN CAMERA OBSCURA

THE CAMERA'S oldest ancestor is called the *camera obscura*. It is a small box that uses light to reproduce the image of an object. Astronomers used the camera obscura to study the sun without hurting their eyes. Artists used it to help them draw or paint outdoors.

In Latin, the phrase *camera obscura* means *dark room*. At first, cameras obscura really were dark rooms that were only big enough to fit one person. The room took in light from the outside world through a small hole in the wall. When the light hit a viewing screen, it formed an image of whatever was outside of the room. Over time, cameras obscura became smaller and smaller, until they could fit in your hand.

In this activity, you'll use a shoebox to create your own camera obscura!

MATERIALS:

- Shoebox (or a similar-sized cardboard box)
- Black marker
- Retractable utility knife
- Tracing paper
- Scissors
- Duct tape
- Art supplies: paint, markers, crayons, etc.
- Writing materials
- Plain paper (for artwork)

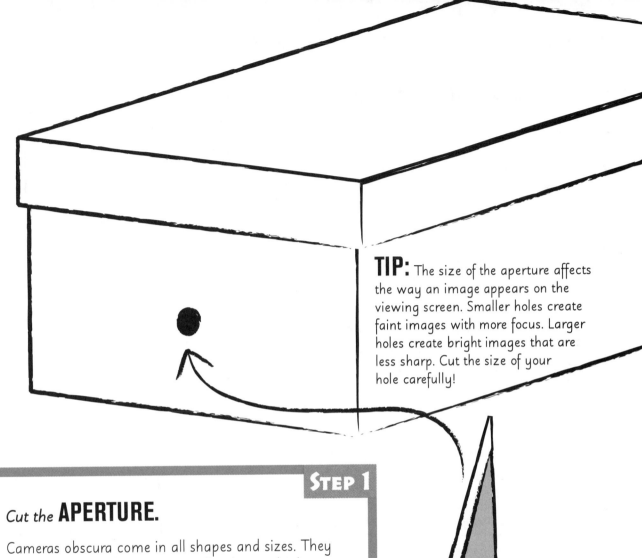

TIP: The size of the aperture affects the way an image appears on the viewing screen. Smaller holes create faint images with more focus. Larger holes create bright images that are less sharp. Cut the size of your hole carefully!

STEP 1

Cut the **APERTURE.**

Cameras obscura come in all shapes and sizes. They can be as big as a room or smaller than a drink can. At any size, a camera obscura has the same basic design. It is always a box with a hole and a viewing screen. That hole is called an *aperture*. It is where light enters the camera obscura.

To make your aperture, draw a circle in the center of one of the short ends of the shoebox. The circle should be about 0.25 inches (0.6 centimeters) in diameter. Ask an adult to cut out the circle with a utility knife. Remove any excess cardboard from around the hole on the inside of the box.

Install the **VIEWING SCREEN.**

All cameras obscura have a viewing screen. The screen can be tiny or the size of a wall. Your viewing screen will be located on the side of the shoebox opposite the aperture.

To make your screen, grab your piece of tracing paper. Place the short side of the shoebox on top of the paper and trace around it to make a rectangle. Cut out the rectangle and set aside.

Next, you'll need to create the window for your viewing screen. Begin by drawing a rectangle onto the side of the shoebox opposite the aperture. Leave at least a 1/2-inch- (1.25 centimeter-) frame around the rectangle. Ask an adult to cut out the rectangle using a utility knife.

Tape the tracing paper rectangle over the window on the shoebox. Make sure it is light-tight. Your viewing screen is now ready for action!

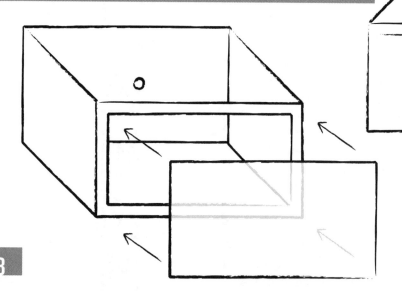

ADD THE *finishing touches.*

Centuries ago, artists used cameras obscura to help them draw or paint different scenes. Small cameras obscura were popular because they were easy to carry from place to place. These portable objects were usually wooden boxes with drawers holding art supplies.

To finish your camera obscura, put the lid on the shoebox and secure it with duct tape. (Make sure that light can't leak through the cracks.) Decorate your camera obscura using markers, paint, or any other materials you choose. For an authentic look, paint a wood-grain pattern. You can even paint fake drawers on the box!

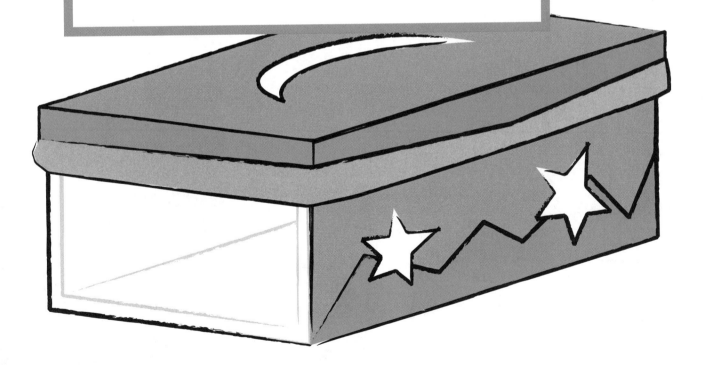

Experiment with different **LIGHT SOURCES.**

Traditionally, artists used natural light from the sun to power cameras obscura. If you are indoors and it's a sunny day, find a room with a big window. (Make sure to open the shades or curtains, if there are any.) Turn off all the lights in the room. Point the aperture of your camera obscura toward the window. You should see an upside-down image of the window on your viewing screen. If the image is faint, try viewing your camera obscura from underneath a blanket. (This will help to block out light.)

Next, experiment with other light sources. You can try flashlights or lamps. Which light source creates more interesting images? Why? Record your observations as you work.

To learn more about the history of the camera, visit: http://bit.ly/cameraobsc

Tip: The images your camera obscura produces will be upside-down. Light reflected from an object enters the camera obscura through the aperture, and produces an image on the inside of the box. Light rays from the top of the object make up the lower part of the image, and those from the bottom form the upper part.

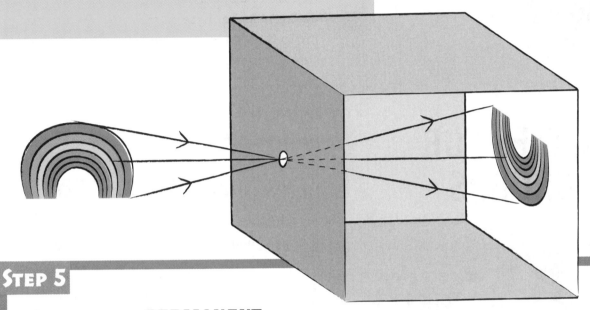

Make the image PERMANENT.

The camera obscura is similar to a film camera. The key difference is that a camera obscura does not have the tools to make a lasting image. And film photographs were not invented until the 1800's. So how did artists make an image permanent?

Before photographs, artists used the camera obscura to help them record permanent images. Some people simply traced the viewing screen. Others used the image in the viewing screen as a guide, which is what you will do now.

Position your camera obscura so that you can see the viewing screen without holding it. (A stack of books on a table makes a good base.) Remember to point the aperture at a light source. Now draw or paint the image you see, using the viewing screen as a reference. When you're finished, take a long look at your artwork. Is your art realistic, like a photograph? Or is it more abstract? Craft an artist's statement by writing a few sentences to explain your artistic choices.

GAMES FOR GROUPS

ARE YOU BORED for no good reason? If you answered yes, then gather a group of family members or friends together and try these fun and wacky games!

Be sure to ask permission from an adult before playing these games. You may need to move some breakable objects and set some safety boundaries before you begin!

Write, Fold, Pass, DRAW, REPEAT!

Break out your pencils and get ready to draw when you play this speedy guessing game!

Make sure each player has a pencil and a big piece of paper. Everyone starts by writing a descriptive sentence at the top of their sheet of paper. The more descriptive your sentences, the better! Here's an example: *The angry elephant and the happy bluebird quickly walked to the coffee shop on the corner.*

Each person hands his or her piece of paper to the player on the left. That person reads the sentence and draws a picture of what is described in the sentence. Next, that person folds over the top of the paper so that the original sentence is hidden but the picture is still visible. They pass the paper to the person on their left.

To watch a video

about a fun party game, visit:
http://bit.ly/groupgames

EVERYBODY'S "IT" *(Tag with a Twist)*

This game is pretty simple, but it's a crowd pleaser. It's just like tag, except every person playing is "it." The game starts when one person says, "Everybody's it!" Then everyone tries to tag one another. If you get tagged, you sit out until the round is over. The last person standing wins!

The person who now has the piece of paper looks at the picture and tries to guess the original sentence. (No peeking!) They write down a sentence, fold the piece of paper over the picture, and pass the paper to the left. The next person reads the new sentence and draws a picture depicting what it says. They then fold the paper over the second sentence and pass the paper to the left.

The game continues in this way until all of the pieces of paper go around the group one time. (Hint: the papers will end up back with the people who wrote the original sentences.) At the end of the game, each person reads his or her original sentence aloud and shows everyone the new sentences and pictures. The fun part is looking at the crazy pictures and seeing how far the new sentences have gone from the original!

Name **PATTERN**

This game is especially fun if you have a group of people. You can use this game to learn everyone's name—or test your memory!

Start by standing or sitting in a circle. One person says his or her name and then makes any kind of a physical gesture, such as waving, hopping up and down, or spinning in a circle. Go around the circle once so each player can establish his or her name and gesture. (Each person should have a different gesture!)

Next, go around the circle again. This time, the first player starts by saying their name and making their gesture. Then they say another person's name and perform that person's gesture. That person repeats their own name and gesture, and then says someone else's name and performs their gesture. Once each player knows everyone else's name, your group can perform only the gestures.

To make this game even harder, play it with your eyes closed! You can play the game the same way, but players make sounds instead of gestures. (Choose any kind of sound, such as an animal noise, whistle, or honk!) Players then have to listen very carefully and remember which name goes with which sound. (It's harder than you might think!)

The Great **MARBLE ROLL**

To begin the game, gather up recycled cardboard tubes from paper toweling or gift-wrapping paper.

Use scissors to cut one cardboard tube in half lengthwise so that you have two pieces, each about 1 foot (0.3 meter) long. These pieces will be the "pathways" for your marble to roll! Repeat this process until you have the same number of pathways as you have players. Give each player a pathway and have the group line up shoulder to shoulder.

The first player takes the marble and releases it on one end of their pathway. Without touching the marble again, the player rolls the marble down the pathway and into the next player's pathway. (Hint: It's okay if the two pathways touch!) That player then rolls the marble on to the next player, and on and on. After each player passes the marble, he or she moves to the end of the line and waits to roll the marble again. If one player drops the marble, they are out. The rest of the group continues rolling and passing the marble until only one person is left standing!

For more of a challenge, time the game at two minutes and see if you can pass the marble around your group four times without dropping it on the floor. You could also try breaking up into two groups and racing to see which group can roll the marble the fastest!

MATERIALS:

- Long cardboard tubes, such as paper towel tubes
- Scissors
- Marble

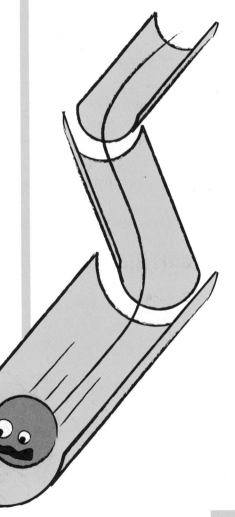

Indoor Foot VOLLEYBALL

Finally your feet are the center of attention in this fun twist on the classic volleyball game. Grab some friends, a balloon, and a pair of socks and get ready to play indoor foot volleyball!

First, find a large play area, blow up the balloon, and make sure every player is wearing a pair of socks. (This will make the balloon easier to kick.) Then, use a long piece of string to divide the play area into two sides. (If you do not have string, you can use pillows, stuffed toys, or any other soft items you choose to separate the sides.) Split the group into two teams and have each player get into a crab-style position on the floor (both hands and feet on the floor with the stomach facing up).

Flip a coin to see which team will serve first. This team tosses the balloon into the air and kicks it over the string to their opponents. Each team kicks the balloon back and forth, using only their feet to touch the balloon. If one team lets the balloon hit the ground or touches the balloon with their hands, the other team gets a point. The team who wins a point restarts the game by serving the balloon. The first team to reach 10 points wins the match! Play several matches to see which team is the indoor foot volleyball champion!

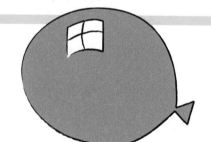

MATERIALS:

- Balloon
- Socks
- String

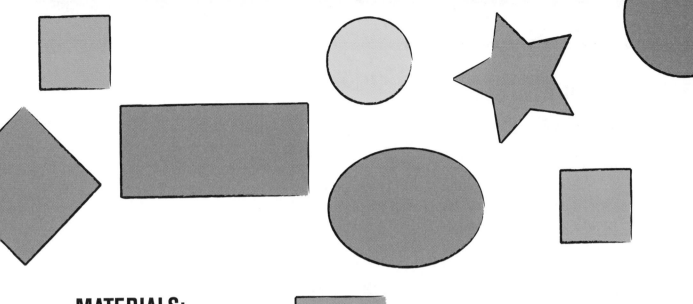

MATERIALS:

- Colored construction paper
- Scissors
- Masking tape

SHAPE *Tangle*

Get ready to twist and shout as you get tangled up in this game! First, cut the colored construction paper into any shapes you choose, such as triangles, squares, and circles. (Hint: The more players you have, the more shapes you will need to cut out.) Next, spread the shapes out on the floor and use masking tape to attach them to the floor. (Ask an adult for permission first!) Pick one player to be the caller. This player has an important job—they will call out directions, such as "Put your right hand on a square," or "Touch your left foot on a circle." (Hint: For more of a challenge, the caller can include the color of the shape, such as "Put your right hand on a yellow square.") The rest of the players must follow these directions and bend and twist to reach several shapes at once. Players who fall down or cannot follow a direction are out of the game. The winning player gets to be the caller for the next round!

INDOOR *Olympic Games*

Invite friends and family members to participate in your very own indoor Olympic games! Have everyone join in to make your own Olympic torch, design medals for the winners, and organize a medals ceremony! Choose from the suggested events below or use your creativity to make up your own Olympic games. You could even select some of the other Games for Groups to include as part of your competition!

Suggested Events:

Relay Hop Race

Divide your group into two equal teams. Decide on your relay race course throughout the house. (For example, the race could begin at the front door, continue through the hallway, around the kitchen, to the family room, and so on until you reach a finish line.) Spread the players out along the route, having one member of each team in each spot. The players will then race one another along the course, hopping on one foot until they tag their teammate, who then hops to the next team member. Continue this hopping relay race until the first team reaches the finish line! Try a longer course, including obstacles, or a timed race for even more of a challenge.

Sock Basketball

Roll a few pairs of socks into balls. Next, find an open play area near a wall. Place an empty laundry basket or waste basket next to the wall. Take seven steps from the basket and mark your spot with masking tape or string. Each player takes turns trying to throw the sock ball in the basket from this distance. (Hint: For an easier game, take three steps back. For more of a challenge, take 10 steps back.) Each basket is worth two points. For the final round, try wacky ways to score a basket, like tossing under your leg, hopping on one foot, and any other fun ideas you come up with. The player who scores the most baskets wins!

Bottle Bowling

Collect 10 empty plastic containers, such as drinking bottles or snack jars. (Hint: The game will be easier if the containers are identical, and more challenging if they are different. Choose the skill level that is best for you!) Set up the bottles vertically in a triangular shape on the ground. Have one player roll a lightweight ball, such as a tennis ball or a soft sponge ball, toward the bottles and see how many he or she can knock down. Each player has two tries to knock down all of the bottles. After two turns, reset the bottles to the triangle shape. The next player then takes a turn. Keep score as you go. The first player to knock down 50 bottles is the winner!

PSYCHIC *Scavenger Hunt*

Test your psychic abilities with this version of a scavenger hunt!

Have one player write a list of five items that can be found in the same room, such as the family room. The items should be out in the open and could be anything, from a cup to a pillow to a dog's toy. Don't let anyone else see the list!

When the list is complete, tell the rest of the group to use their psychic powers to "read" the list and collect the correct items. Each player has two minutes to collect five objects from the room. When time is up, have all of the players return with their chosen items. If anyone brings back an object that is on the original list, they get one point. The player with the most points at the end of the first round gets to make the list for the next round. (Hint: Be sure to have everyone put back the items before the next round begins!) The first player to get 10 points wins!

For more advanced psychics, try limiting the scavenger hunt list to objects that are the same color, or objects that begin with the same letter of the alphabet. Be creative!

Guess THE LEADER

Keep a close eye on your group members as you play this new spin on the game of follow the leader.

To begin, have the entire group stand in a large circle. Choose one player to be the "guesser" and have them leave the room. Once the guesser leaves the room, have the group select a "leader." The leader starts to perform an action, such as swaying from side to side, waving, clapping, or tapping one foot. The rest of the group follows the leader's action. As the group performs the action, call the guesser back into the room and have them stand in the center of the circle. The guesser's job is to try to find the leader.

Here comes the tricky part: The leader can change the action at any time, and the rest of the group should follow the new movement. Changing the motion can help the guesser find the leader, but it can also make the guesser more puzzled. Players can try to confuse the guesser by looking away from the leader. The leader can also try to confuse the guesser by subtly changing the motion when the guesser is not looking at them. The guesser has three chances to name the leader. If they are right, then the leader becomes the guesser in the next round!

Tied in a **HUMAN KNOT**

Try to stay linked to your friends while playing this silly game that will tie you up in knots!

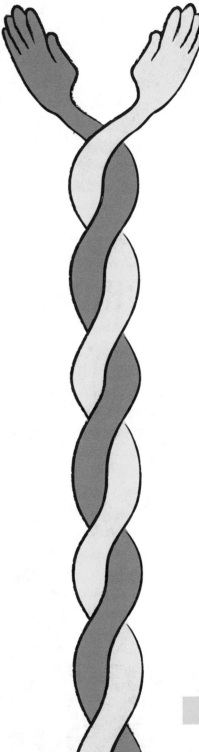

To start, count the number of people in your group. If you have over 10 people, split into two groups. Each group should have an even number of people. (Hint: This game works best if you have 10 or 12 people per group!) Let the group stand shoulder to shoulder in a circle. Have each player reach out their right hand and grasp the hand of someone across the circle from them. Then, everyone takes their left hand and grasps the hand of a different person. Be sure that each player is holding hands with two different people, and that they are not holding hands with the person next to them. Your group is now tied in a human knot!

Now, players should begin to untangle the knot. The trick is that you cannot let go of anyone's hand! You may have to duck under or over someone's arm, crawl under the knot, or even move backward to untangle the knot! Players cannot unclasp and re-clasp hands in order to undo the knot.

The goal is to get the group back into a circle, with everyone holding hands with the people beside them. (Hint: If you are playing with two groups, you can have a race to see which group can undo the knot in the least amount of time. You can also limit the game to five minutes to make it more difficult.) This may seem easy, but you will soon find that it takes a lot of teamwork to untangle a human knot!

BRIDGES are structures that enable people to cross over lakes, rivers, canyons, and highways. When building a bridge, engineers must consider many different factors. How heavy is the bridge? How much weight does the bridge need to carry? How does the bridge look?

In this series of experiments, you will become a bridge engineer. By building a simple straw bridge and adding support structures, you'll discover for yourself what kinds of bridge designs are the strongest!

MATERIALS:

- Box of straight straws
- Scissors
- Tape
- Ruler
- Thin permanent marker
- Thin cardboard, about 4 inches (10 centimeters) tall by 8 ¼ inches (21 centimeters) wide
- Paper cup
- Measuring cups
- 3 cups of dried beans
- Two stacks of books, each 2 inches (5 centimeters) thick
- Pencil
- Notebook

CONSTRUCT A GAP *for your bridge to cross.*

For this series of experiments, you will arrange a 12-inch- (30.5-centimeter-) gap between two supports, called *abutments*. The distance between abutments is known as the bridge's *span*.

Use two stacks of books as your abutments. Each stack should be 2 inches (5 centimeters) thick. Set the stacks 12 inches (30.5 centimeters) apart on a table or the floor. This is the obstacle your bridge must cross. Next, you'll make a simple bridge to cross the span.

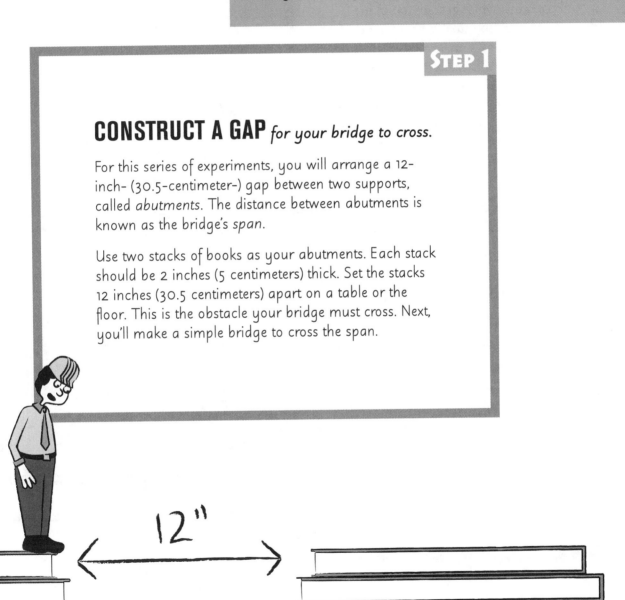

Construct a **SIMPLE BRIDGE.**

The main structure of any bridge is the beams, which rest on top of the abutments. To make a beam, pinch the end of one straw and stick it inside another straw. Repeat this step with a third straw. Slide the straws together until they measure a total of 14 inches (35.5 centimeters). Wrap tape around the spots where the straws join together to keep them from slipping.

3" 7" 11"

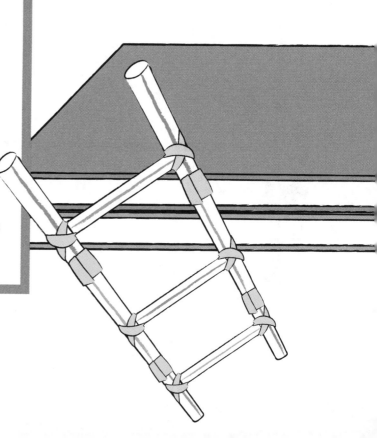

Repeat these steps to make a second straw beam. Measure and mark points at 3, 7, and 11 inches (8, 18, and 28 centimeters) on each beam.

To connect the beams, cut three 4-inch (10-centimeter) pieces of straw. Tape the straw pieces to your beams at the three points you marked. Your finished simple bridge should resemble a ladder with three rungs.

Place the simple straw bridge across the gap. You now have a simple bridge that's strong enough to support its own weight.

Test your BRIDGE.

How well can your bridge handle added weight? Find out by testing it. Cut a piece of thin cardboard 4 inches by 8 ¼-inches (10 centimeters by 21 centimeters). Place it over the width of the bridge.

Place a paper cup on the piece of cardboard in the center of the bridge. Now you're ready to find out how much weight your bridge can hold.

Measure ½ cup of beans. Pour the beans into the paper cup. How far does the bridge bend? Measure the space between the lowest point of the bridge and the bottom of the gap. Subtract this measurement from the total height of 2 inches (5 centimeters) to determine how far the bridge bends.

How many cups of beans can the simple bridge hold before it bends so low that it touches the bottom of the gap?

Record your bridge experiments in a notebook. Make a drawing of your bridge, and note any changes you make to its design as you test it.

Record the results of the weight tests. Compare these results to determine which designs work best for building bridges.

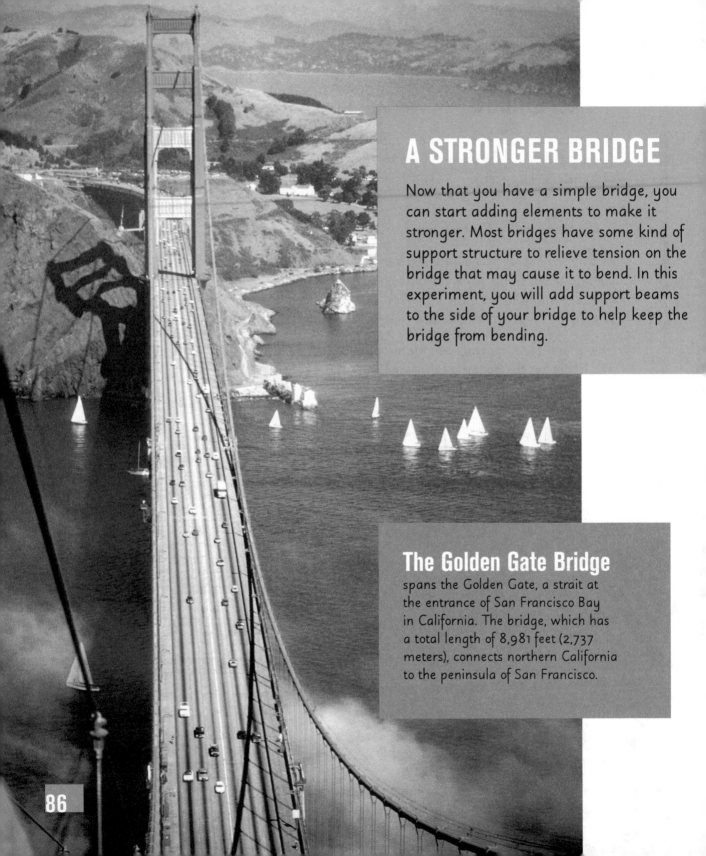

A STRONGER BRIDGE

Now that you have a simple bridge, you can start adding elements to make it stronger. Most bridges have some kind of support structure to relieve tension on the bridge that may cause it to bend. In this experiment, you will add support beams to the side of your bridge to help keep the bridge from bending.

The Golden Gate Bridge

spans the Golden Gate, a strait at the entrance of San Francisco Bay in California. The bridge, which has a total length of 8,981 feet (2,737 meters), connects northern California to the peninsula of San Francisco.

Construct **SUPPORT BEAMS.**

Construct two additional 14-inch (35.5-centimeter) straw beams. On each beam, measure and mark four points at 1, 5, 9, and 13 inches (2.5, 13, 23, and 33 centimeters).

Cut eight 4-inch (10-centimeter) pieces of straw (four for each support beam). Tape one end of the straw pieces to each of the four points you marked on each support beam.

Next, tape the open ends of the straw pieces to the simple bridge beams. Your finished support-beam bridge should resemble two parallel 4-rung ladders connected on each side of your original bridge.

Tips for Making a Strong Bridge: Truss Construction

Some shapes work better than others to support a structure's weight. The triangle is a strong shape for building. It can withstand great pressure pushing down on it, which makes it the ideal shape to carry the weight of a bridge. Bridge frameworks composed of triangles are called *trusses*.

Try adding triangles to the structure of your bridge. Attach diagonal lengths of straw between the sections on the sides of your bridge to add more support. How much stronger does this make your bridge?

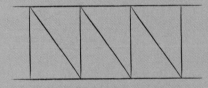

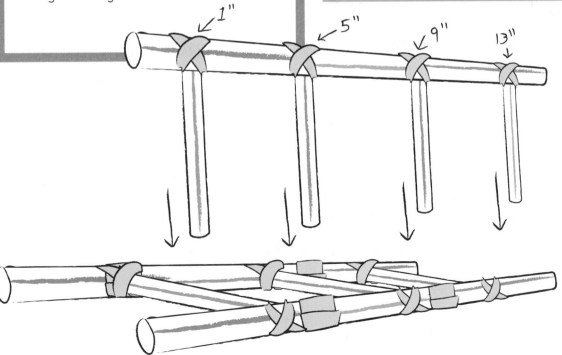

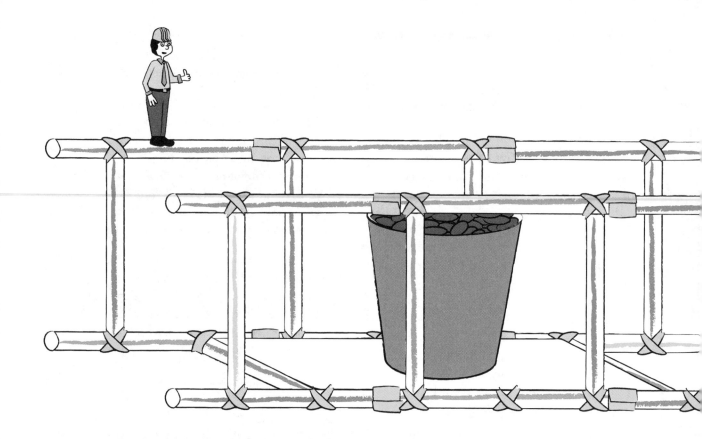

STEP 5

Test the **SUPPORT BEAMS.**

Place the thin cardboard over the width of the bridge. Place the paper cup on the piece of cardboard in the center of the bridge.

Measure ½ cup of beans. Pour them into the paper cup.

How far does the support beam bridge bend? How many cups of beans can the support beam bridge hold before it bends so low that it touches the bottom of the gap?

STEP 6

Design and build your own **BRIDGE.**

Using what you've learned, play with the design of your bridge to strengthen the structure. Try new designs for making your bridge stronger. Look up examples of famous bridges to see how they were constructed. Can you use any of these ideas in your straw bridge design?

Enter the World Book STRAW BRIDGE CONTEST!

World Book is looking for an engineer to build a straw bridge! A prize will be awarded to the engineer who designs, builds, and demonstrates the strongest straw bridge. The bridge must meet the following requirements:

- The bridge span must be 12 inches (30.5 centimeters).
- The bridge must be a single-span bridge. The bridge can be held up only by the abutments on either end.
- The abutments should be 2 inches (5 centimeters) above a table, floor, or other flat surface. Abutments can be books, wood, or anything that raises the bridge 2 inches above the flat surface.
- The bridge cannot be attached to the abutments. (You should be able to pick the bridge up.)
- The bridge must be at least 4 inches (10 centimeters) wide.
- You can use no more than 20 straws to build the bridge, as well as a small piece of thin cardboard to support a paper cup for measurement.
- The bridge must be able to hold at least 2 cups of dry beans.
- The bridge cannot dip so low that it touches the flat surface.

Can you design and build a bridge this strong or even stronger? Submit a video of your straw bridge to World Book!

In the video, explain the design of your bridge and how it makes the bridge strong.

Be sure to show the measurements and demonstrate how many cups of beans your bridge can hold.

World Book science editors will award a prize to the engineer of the strongest straw bridge. Good luck!

To learn more
about the contest, visit:
http://bit.ly/strawbrid

CAN YOU MAKE water rise without touching it? Sure you can! All you need is a jar, a candle, a plate, a match, and a little knowledge of physics!

In this activity, you'll learn about what happens to air when it is heated and cooled.

CANDLE "MAGIC" TRICK

CAUTION!

Ask an adult to help you with this experiment. Be sure to place the candles on saucers, and keep them at a safe distance from you and any flammable materials. Never use candles or matches on your own!

MATERIALS:

- 6 candles (You can use votive, taper, or birthday candles.)
- 3 large saucers, plates, or shallow bowls
- Modeling clay (about a handful)
- 3 large clear glass jars (The jars must be wide enough to fit 3 candles and large enough to hold 1 to 2 liters of water.)
- Food coloring
- Water
- Measuring cup
- Matches or lighter
- Camera, video camera, and/or writing materials

POSITION *the candle.*

Use the modeling clay to secure one candle in the center of a saucer. Make sure the candle is firmly held by the modeling clay. (It shouldn't wobble.) Set the saucer on a flat workspace, such as a table or counter.

Pour the **WATER.**

Put a few drops of food coloring into a measuring cup filled with water. Pour the water into the saucer until it is almost full. The water should surround the candle in the center.

LIGHT *the candle.*

Ask an adult to light the candle. Place a large glass jar over the lit candle. The jar should completely cover the candle and rest on the water-filled saucer. (If there is any space between the jar and the saucer, the experiment won't work.) Watch carefully! Record your observations.

What happened when you placed the jar over the candle? You probably noticed that the flame went out and the jar filled with water. Why do you think this happened? Write down your hypothesis.

TA DA!

POOF!

MODIFY *the experiment.*

Repeat steps 1 through 3, this time placing two candles in the center of the second saucer and three candles in the center of the third saucer.

What do you notice? Does using more candles change the results? How?

Record your observations.

WHAT IS HAPPENING?

The glass jar with three candles should have more water inside it than the other two jars. To understand why, let's take a closer look at what's happening.

When the candle is lit, heat from the flame causes air inside the jar to expand. The space inside the jar is limited, so air gets pushed out as it expands. After you lit your candles, did you see air bubbles rising from underneath the glass? The bubbles are air escaping from the jar. This is similar to what happens when a lid bounces over a pot of boiling water.

The flame needs fuel (the candle wax) and oxygen in order to burn. Since the air inside the jar is limited, most of the oxygen is quickly used up. When the oxygen level gets too low, the flame begins to go out. Then the air inside the jar cools and contracts (shrinks). The water from the saucer moves inside the jar to fill the space left by the shrinking air.

The more candles you use, the hotter the air inside the jar gets. The hotter the air gets, the more it expands. This causes more air to get pushed out of the jar, creating even more space inside the jar for the water to fill. That's why the jar with three candles has the most water.

Further Investigation
Dive deeper into this activity by experimenting with different-sized jars. Record your observations for each jar.

To watch a video
of this experiment, visit: http://bit.ly/candlemagic

MYTHOLOGICAL MONSTER QUEST

MYTHOLOGY is a collection of stories told to explain the mysteries of the world. In early times, questions like "Where did people first come from?" and "Why do the seasons change?" did not have scientific answers. Instead, people told stories that tried to answer these questions. These myths were important to social and religious life.

Myths are also great adventure stories that feature fantastic monsters, gods, and other beings with supernatural powers. Mythological beings can appear human and have human feelings. These stories show human behavior as well as wild adventure and mystery.

In this activity, you are a god who has been turned into ice and is being held at sea by Scylla (*SIHL uh*), a female monster, and her three sisters, the Gorgons. Luckily, the Graeae (*GREE ee*) are three sisters who are on your side. They have snuck a letter and a map of your location to your friend. If your friend chooses to accept the quest to save you and succeeds before you melt, you will grant your friend a special reward!

MATERIALS:

- Modeling clay
- Obstacle-course materials (blankets, pillows, obstructions, toy monsters, dolls, etc.)
- Paper
- Permanent marker
- Tea bags or coffee grounds
- Tablespoon
- Shallow tub or sink
- Drawing and painting supplies
- Ice cube or kitchen timer
- Cup, bowl, or other container
- Camera, video camera, and/or writing materials

STEP 1

PLAN *the quest!*

Make a clay sculpture of yourself as a divine being. You can choose to look like a human, an animal, or a monster. Next, determine the location of Ogygia, the island at sea where you are being held captive. Ogygia can be your house or an area outside. (Be sure to get permission from an adult before choosing an area.) Turn Ogygia into an obstacle course by arranging obstructions and monsters (toys or dolls). Don't forget to include Scylla and the three Gorgons! Hide the sculpture of yourself within Ogygia.

STEP 2

MAP *the quest!*

Once you have arranged Ogygia, you can map the quest! Using a permanent marker and paper, draw a map showing directions through Ogygia to the sculpture. Your map should include distances (measured in footsteps) and symbols that show dangers, such as obstacles and monsters. Be sure to include a map key (a box that names the symbols shown on the map).

To make the map look antique, soak it in water with a few tea bags or a tablespoon of coffee grounds. When the paper has turned light brown, remove it from the water. Once the map has dried, you can make it look even older by crumpling it up, rubbing it on a rough surface, and tearing the edges and corners.

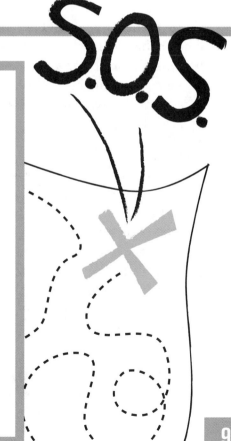

CHALLENGE *the hero or heroine!*

Write a letter to your friend (the hero or heroine) that explains:

Where you are:	*Ogygia*
Who captured you:	*Scylla*
Who guards you:	*Gorgons*
What happened to you:	*Turned into ice*
What hero/heroine must do:	*Rescue you*
The reward for success:	*Hero/heroine becomes a divine being*
The result of failure:	*You melt, hero/heroine is captured*

(You can change any or all of these answers to create a different quest.)

Create an honor or reward for your friend if he or she succeeds. If your friend will become a divine being, choose which divine being he or she will become. Draw a certificate to award your friend the title of divine being.

Create the ice clock. This is a special container to hold an ice cube, such as a cup or a bowl. Explain to your friend that when the ice cube melts, his or her time is up. (Note: if you perform this activity indoors, use a kitchen timer instead. You may wish to give your friend five minutes or more to complete the quest, depending on its level of difficulty.)

Greek mythology
Scylla, Gorgons and Graeae

In Greek mythology, Scylla is a female monster that snatches sailors from their ships at sea. The Gorgons are three sisters (Stheno, Euryale, and Medusa) who have snakes for hair and faces so horrible that anyone who looks at them turns to stone. The Graeae are three aged sisters who have one eye and one tooth among them.

To learn more about Scylla and the Gorgons, visit: http://bit.ly/mythmonster

STEP 4

START *the quest!*

Give the letter and map to your friend. After your friend reads the letter and accepts the quest, take him or her to the entrance of Ogygia. Start the ice clock by placing an ice cube in the special container. Keep an eye on the ice clock throughout the quest! Your friend must now use your map to avoid the dangers and find your sculpture before the ice clock melts.

REWARD *the hero or heroine!*

If your sculpture is found before the time is up, present your friend with the certificate or other special reward.

If your friend has not found your sculpture in time (the ice clock melts), your friend is captured. He or she must now plan a quest for you to solve!

STEP 6

REVERSE *the quest!*

Have your friend plan a quest for you to complete as the hero or heroine. Your friend can use the same story, or together you can look up different myths to create a new story.

DOCUMENT *your quest!*

During the project, document the process through one or more of the following: photography, video, drawing, graphing, writing, cartooning, music writing, or lyric writing.

Interview your friend about their quest and write down his or her answers. Together, write the story of the quest for future readers. Draw pictures of scenes from the quest. Use the same antique process on the story that you used to age the map. This will make your story appear as if it were written in the distant past!

Create your own mythology!

You can also create your own mythological characters or creatures. What are their supernatural powers? Do they look like humans, animals, or monsters? Draw and name your mythological characters. You and your friend can create myths using your own characters as well as existing mythological beings!

CATAPULT LAUNCH

A CATAPULT is a big machine used to throw objects over a long distance. Catapults were first used by warriors in ancient times. Later, in the Middle Ages, soldiers used catapults during castle sieges.

Medieval castles were hard to attack. The walls were high and made of stone. Fighters weren't strong enough to throw things over the walls with their bare hands. Instead, they used catapults like giant slingshots. With catapults, heavy stones and other items whizzed over castle walls.

For this activity, you will build your own mini catapult. It will be small, but powerful—the objects you launch will fly up to 20 feet (6 meters)!

MATERIALS:

- 9 wooden craft sticks
- 4 rubber bands
- 1 plastic bottle cap (from a recycled bottle of water or soda)
- Craft glue or hot glue
- Recyclable materials (to launch): marshmallows, dried pasta, wadded balls of paper, etc.
- Measuring tape
- Notebook and pen or pencil

Catapults were used by warriors from ancient times through the Middle Ages to attack walled cities and castles. In this illustration, soldiers use a catapult during a castle siege.

START BUILDING *your catapult.*

The catapults used during castle attacks were very large machines made of wood and rope. You'll use two stacks of craft sticks to build your catapult. First, form a tall stack with seven of the craft sticks. To secure the tall stack, wrap one rubber band around each end.

Now make a short stack with the remaining two craft sticks. Secure just one end of the short stack with a rubber band.

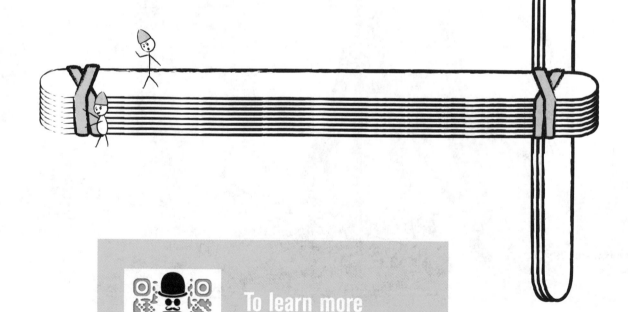

To learn more
about castles, visit:
http://bit.ly/catlaunch

Finish the **ASSEMBLY.**

A catapult is actually a simple machine called a *lever*. Every lever has a special point called a *fulcrum*. Your catapult's fulcrum will be the place where the stacks of sticks cross.

To create your fulcrum, lift one of the craft sticks in the short stack. Carefully slide the tall stack between the two sticks. When you can't slide the tall stack any farther, secure it in place with the last rubber band. Refer to the diagrams as you work to make sure you're on the right track.

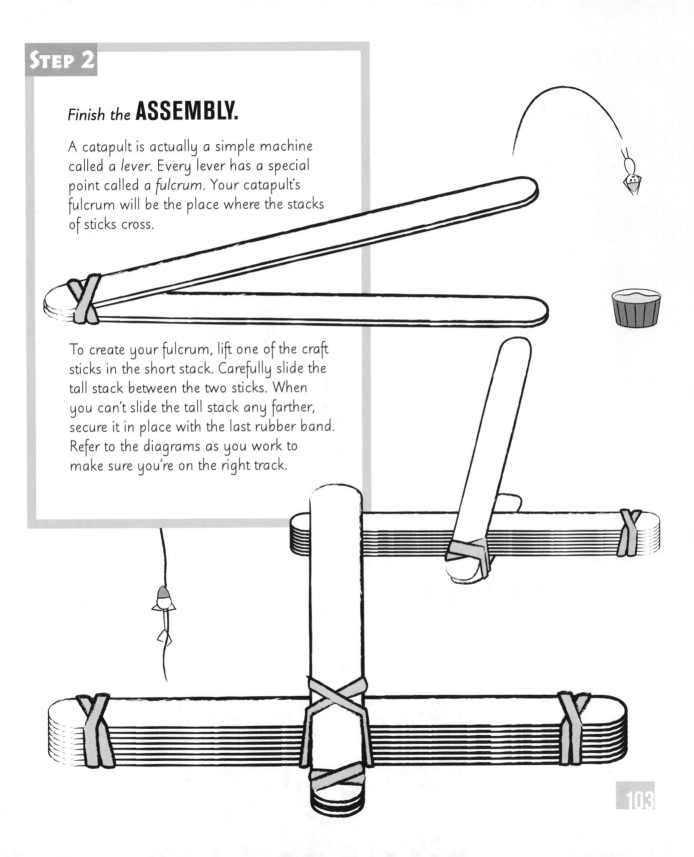

Prepare to **LAUNCH.**

In the Middle Ages, some catapults had a special basket on one end. This basket was used as a loading zone. It held objects before they were launched.

Since your catapult is small, your "basket" will be a plastic bottle cap. Glue the top of the cap near the tip of the top stick. (Make sure you leave enough space at the tip of the stick to place your fingertip.) Give the glue time to dry before you move on to the next step.

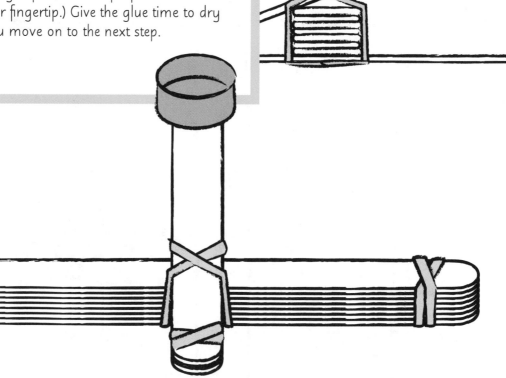

Throughout the project,

document the process with photography, video, drawing, graphing, writing, cartooning, music writing, or any other form.

STEP 4

Let it **FLY!**

During castle attacks, fighters used catapults to launch dangerous objects like flaming spears and stones. These objects were called *projectiles* because they soared through the air. Defenders inside the castle could launch things over the walls and into the crowd below. Invaders outside the castle could also hurl things up and over the tall walls.

For safety, your projectiles should be soft and light. Make sure your launch zone is clear of anything fragile. (You might want to go outside so you'll have plenty of room.) Place a marshmallow or another projectile in the cap. Slowly push down on the tip of the stick with your fingertip. As you push, tension builds. Remove your fingertip to release the tension. Your projectile will take off! Use a measuring tape to see how far it flew through the air.

Now repeat the process with your other projectiles. Try changing your catapult to see how it affects your results. You could place the catapult on a book or another base to change the launch angle. Next, try moving the fulcrum. What happens when you move the tall stack of sticks up or down the launching arm? What happens if you throw the projectiles instead of using the catapult? Take notes as you go.

Watch out!

Medieval soldiers used catapults like this one to launch such threatening materials as sharp spears, heavy stones, rotting matter, and even burning wood or sand! This type of catapult sent materials flying up to 1,300 feet (396 meters) away!

THIS END UP

Have some extra time?

Ask a friend to build a makeshift castle from cardboard, blocks, or blankets. Then, use your catapult to launch your projectiles over the wall!

THIS END UP

A ZIP LINE is a cable that people use to get from one place to another. At first, zip lines were probably used for transportation, especially in mountainous areas. More recently, zip lines have been part of the tourist industry. People on vacation like to see the sights from a different point of view.

In this activity, you will harness the forces of gravity and friction to build your own zip line. You'll send an action figure whizzing down the line on different adventures to figure out which set-up works best!

MATERIALS:

- String, dental floss, or fishing line
- Plastic drinking straw
- Scissors
- Duct tape
- Rubber band
- Action figure
- Clothespin
- Camera (or art supplies) and writing materials

SCOUT *a location.*

All zip lines have the same basic design. The line begins at a high point and slopes downward to a low point. The downward slope helps gravity move riders down the zip line. Zip lines that are short with a sharp slope move more quickly. Zip lines that are long with a gentle slope move more slowly.

Your first task is to find a safe place to put your zip line so people won't walk into it and get hurt. Find a high spot where the line will start. Anything tall and sturdy will work. (If you're inside, try a rack or a hook. Outside, a branch is a good bet.) Ask an adult to tie the line to the high spot.

Next, stretch the line to a place where you can anchor it. Remember that the angle should slope downward. Your zip line will work best if you choose a moveable anchor, such as a chair or table leg. That way, you can move the anchor to make your line taut (pulled tight).

Before you cut the line, make sure you have enough line to tie it to your anchor. **Do NOT tie the bottom of the line yet!**

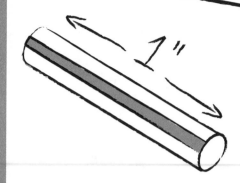

Prepare the HANDLES AND HARNESS.

In addition to the line itself, zip lines use a simple machine called a *pulley*. A pulley is a wheel over which a rope is passed. Pulleys reduce friction, which helps riders move quickly down the line.

Since your zip line will not support a real person, you won't need a pulley. Instead, you'll make a simple harness using a straw, rubber band, and duct tape. Start by trimming a 1-inch (2.5-centimeter) piece from the straw. (Throw away the remainder.)

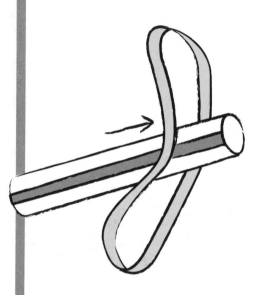

Loop the rubber band around the straw. Now tape the middle of the rubber band to the straw so that two loops hang down on either side. (See the illustrations on this page for reference.) These loops will serve as the harness for your action figure.

Thread the line through the straw. Move the straw all the way up to the top of the line. Clamp one side of the straw with the clothespin to prevent it from sliding down the zip line. Finally, tie the bottom of the line to its anchor. Make sure the line is taut.

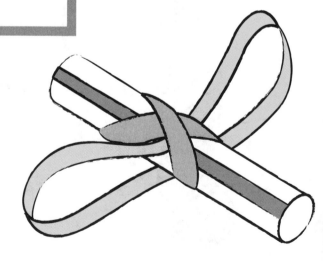

To learn more about this experiment, visit:
http://bit.ly/zipchallenge

GET READY *to launch.*

Before you send your action figure down the zip line, give it a backstory. What is its name? Is it on vacation, at work, or at war? Is the zip line an escape route or is it heading into an ambush? Do you think the figure feels nervous, excited, or brave?

Once you have a good story in place, secure your action figure in its harness. To do this, wrap the rubber band loops around the figure's arms, as pictured.

When you're ready to launch, release the straw by squeezing open the clothespin. Note how quickly the figure moves down the zip line. Is it a smooth ride, or are there bumps? What happens at the end of the line? Record your observations.

Ziplining is a popular activity in many scenic tourist destinations. In forests, zipliners can enjoy the view from the height of the tree canopy!

Experiment with **YOUR SETUP.**

Many different factors affect the way your zip line operates. The material you use to make the line, the weight of the action figure, the tension of the line, and the length of the line are all things you can change.

Experiment with your setup by changing one factor at a time. For example, if you used string to make your first zip line, replace it with dental floss for the second round. Choose a different location for the third try. You could also change the length of the straw.

Think about how each change affects your zip line and take notes as you go. After four or five tries, decide which zip line worked best. If someone asked you for advice about how to set up their zip line, what would you say? Write your advice on a sheet of paper.

For a real challenge, try to design a new rig using a pulley!

Throughout the project, document the process with photography, video, drawing, graphing, writing, cartooning, music writing, or any other form.

VOLCANO ERUPTION!

VOLCANOES are one of Earth's most dramatic natural forces. Some volcanoes cause fire, gas, and lava to shoot high into the air. While eruptions can be amazing to watch, they can also be very dangerous. Volcanoes may create huge clouds of hot ash, fast-moving mud slides, and rivers of molten rock that can cause much destruction.

In this activity, you will build your own volcano. Then you'll set off a chemical reaction that will cause it to erupt!

MATERIALS:

- Small jar (no lid necessary)
- Newspaper
- Tray
- Modeling clay (see recipe on page 116)
- Twigs, grass, moss, or rocks (for decoration)
- Water
- Food coloring (optional)
- Liquid dish soap
- Baking soda
- Measuring spoons
- Measuring cup (with spout for easy pouring)
- Distilled white vinegar

As a volcano

erupts, ash, gases, and molten rock from deep underground pour from an opening called a vent.

To watch a video

about volcanoes, visit:
http://bit.ly/eruptvolcano

BUILD *your volcano.*

Close your eyes and picture a volcano. You might imagine a tall mountain with steep sides. Actually, there are many different types of volcanoes. They come in all shapes and sizes. In this activity, you will build a *shield volcano*. The word *shield* refers to the volcano's shape. It looks like the gentle curve of a warrior's shield.

Volcanoes tend to make messes when they erupt. Spread plenty of newspaper on a table or the floor before you begin. (If it's a nice day, you can build your volcano outside.) Place a tray in the center of the newspapers. Then place the jar in the middle of the tray. Use the modeling clay to build your volcano around the jar. (Look at the picture as you go. Remember, a shield volcano is wide with a gentle curve.) Make sure you don't cover the opening of the jar.

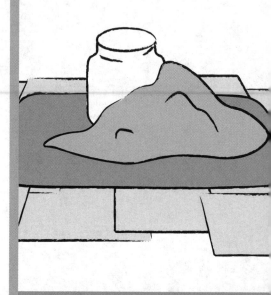

Make Your Own **MODELING CLAY.**

Did you know that you can make your own modeling clay? All you need are a few simple ingredients. This recipe makes about a cup of modeling clay. (If you need more, you can double the recipe.) Don't forget to use food coloring or glitter to make each batch unique!

INGREDIENTS:

1 1/4 cups flour
1/3 cup salt
1/2 cup water
2 teaspoons vegetable oil
Large bowl
Food coloring or glitter (optional)

DIRECTIONS:

Combine the flour and the salt in a large bowl. Add the water and the vegetable oil and stir for 30 seconds. Once the dough has come together, knead it with your hands. Continue to knead the dough until it's smooth. (This may take a few minutes.) Add a few drops of food coloring or glitter. Work it through the dough with your fingers.

Create the **LANDSCAPE.**

Earth's shell consists of many pieces called *plates*. Most volcanoes form along the edges of these plates. Volcanoes can also form at places called *hot spots*, which can be far away from plate edges. Most shield volcanoes form at hot spots.

To create the landscape for your volcano, decorate it with natural materials. You can use items you find outside, such as twigs, grass, moss, and rocks. When you're finished, give your volcano a name. Some volcanoes have names that describe how they look. Others are named after people or gods. You can even name your volcano after yourself!

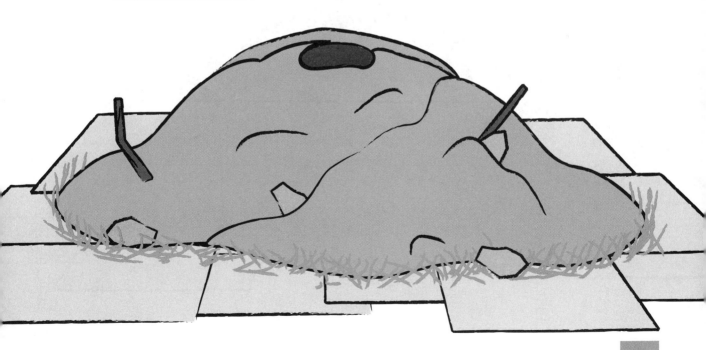

Prepare THE MAGMA.

Volcanic eruptions are caused by magma. Magma is hot liquid rock. It is deep below the ground. Over time, magma rises toward Earth's surface. It collects in a chamber below (or inside) the volcano. As the magma collects, pressure builds.

To make your magma, place 1 tablespoon of water in the jar. Add a few drops of food coloring and a squirt of liquid dish soap. Add 2 teaspoons of baking soda. Finally, place 2 tablespoons of vinegar in the measuring cup. Set it aside until you're ready for action.

Watch the **ERUPTION.**

Eruptions happen when magma reaches Earth's surface. The magma chamber breaks open when the pressure becomes too high. As soon as the magma hits the air, it's called *lava*. Lava is very hot. It can be up to 12 times hotter than boiling water!

To turn your magma into lava, carefully pour the vinegar into the jar. When the vinegar touches the baking soda, a chemical reaction will occur. The reaction produces gas that will cause the lava to rise. The dish soap makes the lava extra foamy.

Your eruption will happen very quickly, so pay close attention! How long does it last? How much lava did it create? Record your observations as you go.

Throughout the project, document the process with photography, video, drawing, graphing, writing, cartooning, music writing, or any other form.

MAKE YOUR OWN VOCAL CORDS

WE USE our vocal cords, muscles, and lungs in many combinations throughout the day. One of the ways these three parts work together is to create your voice. When air from the lungs passes through the vibrating vocal cords in the throat, your voice comes to life! When you speak, you stretch and relax your vocal cords to produce different kinds of sounds. In this activity, you will make a model of human vocal cords to better understand how your voice makes certain sounds.

MATERIALS:

- Several plastic cups of different sizes
- Several rubber bands of different thicknesses

What are VOCAL CORDS?

The vocal cords are two small folds of elastic tissue that stretch along the sides of an air passage at the top of the throat. This air passage is called the *larynx (LAR ihngks)*.

The larynx lies between the back of the tongue and a tube in the throat called the *trachea (TRAY kee uh)*. The trachea carries air between the lungs and the nose and mouth.

When you breathe, your relaxed vocal cords form a wide, V-shaped opening that lets air

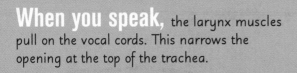
When you speak, the larynx muscles pull on the vocal cords. This narrows the opening at the top of the trachea.

RELAXED VOCAL CORDS FOR BREATHING

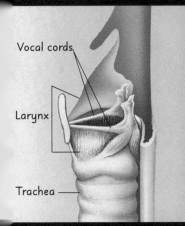

Vocal cords

Larynx

Trachea

TENSED VOCAL CORDS FOR SPEAKING

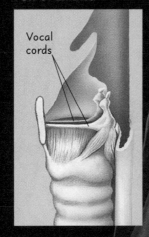

Vocal cords

pass between the lungs and the head. When you speak, your muscles pull tightly on the vocal cords and narrow the opening.

Air moving from the lungs through the larynx causes your tightened vocal cords to vibrate. These vibrations produce sounds. The more tightly the vocal cords are stretched, the higher the sounds we produce. The more relaxed our cords are, the lower the sounds we make. We call these sounds our voice.

Each person's voice has a different *pitch,* or highness or lowness of sound. The size of the larynx and the thickness and tension of the vocal cords determine the pitch of a person's voice. Since each person has a different set of vocal cords, everyone's voice sounds a little different!

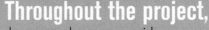

Throughout the project, document the process with photography, video, drawing, graphing, writing, cartooning, music writing, or any other form.

121

Construct the **VOCAL CORDS.**

Choose one rubber band and one plastic cup. Stretch the rubber band all the way around the top and bottom of the cup. The cup represents the larynx and the rubber band represents the vocal cords.

To watch a video about vocal cords, visit: http://bit.ly/vocalcords

STEP 2

Create **VIBRATIONS.**

Flick the top of the rubber band with your finger to make it vibrate. The vibration produces a sound. The size and shape of the cup, as well as the thickness and tension of the rubber band, determine the pitch of the sound made. Together, the larynx and vocal cords create the voice's unique *timbre*, or quality of sound.

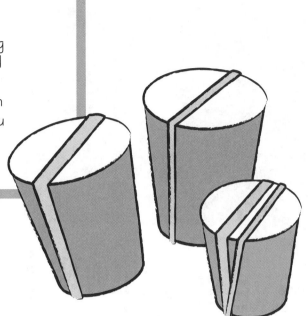

ALTER *the cords.*

You can produce different sounds by altering the vocal cords. Try pulling the rubber band tighter around the cup as you flick it. What happened to the pitch? It should have gotten higher. What happens to the pitch when you relax the rubber band?

Did you know?

As children, boys and girls have about the same-sized vocal cords. But as boys grow up, their voices become lower. This happens when a boy's larynx grows larger and the vocal cords grow longer and thicker. Women's vocal cords do not grow as much as men's, so their voices usually stay at a higher pitch.

STEP 4

Experiment with THE MATERIALS.

You can also change the sound by experimenting with the materials you use. Try using different-size cups with different thicknesses of rubber bands. Mix and match the cups with the rubber bands, and try all of the possible combinations. What do you think will happen if you use a thicker rubber band on a small cup? How will the sounds change? Write down your predictions and then test them to find out if you are on the right track!

WHEN YOU ARE AT HOME in your bedroom, do you know which way is north? How would you know if your window faced south? In both cases, a compass could help you find your way. A compass is an instrument for showing direction. In this activity, you'll learn how to make your own compass!

A simple compass uses a magnetized needle that points to the nearest *magnetic pole*. Magnetic poles are the opposite ends of a magnet. These ends are called north and south poles.

The planet Earth is like a giant magnet. It has two magnetic poles. If you live north of the equator, a compass needle will point toward Earth's North Pole. If you live south of the equator, the needle will point toward the South Pole. This makes it easy to determine which way is north, south, east, or west. These four directions are called the *cardinal directions*.

You can make your own compass in a few easy steps.

MATERIALS:

- Sewing needle
- Magnet
- Wine cork
- Bread knife
- Cutting board
- Permanent marker
- Glass jar
- Camera, video camera, and/or writing materials

A pocket compass has a magnetic needle that points north. People use a pocket compass to find their way when there are no landmarks to guide them.

STEP 1

MAGNETIZE *the needle.*

Rub the needle with the magnet, making sure to rub in just one direction. (Needles are sharp, so be careful!)

This will magnetize the needle.

STEP 2

POSITION *the needle.*

Ask an adult to use a bread knife to cut a round slice from the wine cork. The slice should be about the width of a pencil.

Lay the cork slice flat on the cutting board. Push the magnetized needle through the side of the cork. The needle should stick out each side of the cork.

125

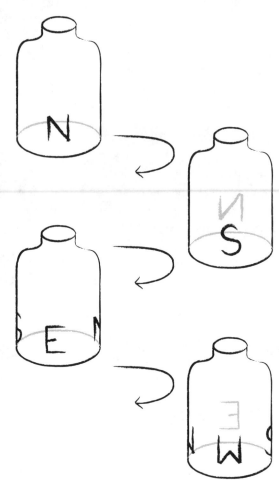

Label THE JAR.

With the permanent marker, write a big N (for north) on one side of the glass jar.

Turn the jar until the N is on the opposite side and mark an S (for south).

Now turn the jar halfway with the N on the right side and S on the left. Halfway between the N and S, write an E (for east).

Now, with the jar turned so the N is on the left and S on the right, write a W (for west). The E and W should line up, as should the N and S.

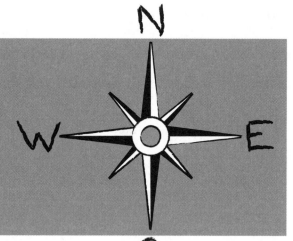

Early Compasses

The first compasses were simple pieces of magnetic iron, usually floated on straw or cork in a bowl of water—similar to the compass you are creating! Earth's magnetic field would cause the piece of iron to point roughly toward the North Pole. Later compass designs looked more like clocks. These designs have a rotating magnetic needle and a surface called a compass card. The compass card is labeled with letters that stand for the cardinal directions.

FIND *your direction.*

Fill the jar about halfway with water. Set it on a flat surface.

Float the cork and needle in the water.

After it finishes turning, the sharp end of the needle should point north (or south, if you live south of the equator).

Once the needle lines up with the N (or S) on the glass, you can now tell which direction is north, south, east, and west.

You've made your own compass! Now you can lead the way!

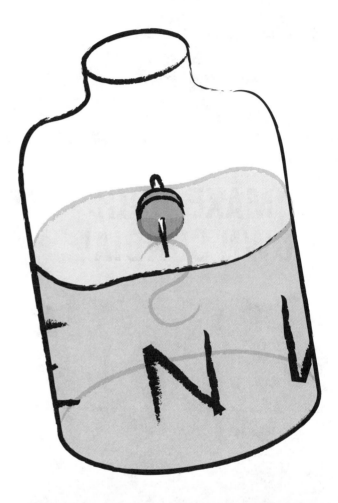

To learn more about
the history of the compass, visit:
http://bit.ly/makecompass

Throughout the project, document the process with photography, video, drawing, graphing, writing, cartooning, music writing, or any other form.

MAKE YOUR OWN SUNDIAL

DID YOU KNOW that you can tell time using shadows? No, it's not a magic trick. All you need is a device called a *sundial*.

Most of the clocks we use today need electric power. But thousands of years ago, electric power didn't exist. Instead of wall clocks and watches, people used sundials.

In the ancient world, sundials helped people know when it was time to pray. Since then, technology has advanced so much that we've placed a sundial on the planet Mars!

For this activity, you will make your own sundial using simple materials. Make sure you choose a bright, sunny day. (Sundials don't work when it's gray and gloomy.) And make sure to start this project early in the morning, right after you wake up.

The materials list for this activity assumes up to 12 hours of daylight. During summer, daylight may last more than 12 hours in some regions. You can add or subtract the number of flowerpots you use based on the hours of sunlight expected on the day you create your sundial.

MATERIALS:

- 13 flowerpots, or 1 flowerpot and 12 large flat stones
- Painting supplies
- Dirt, sand, or rocks (enough to fill one flowerpot)
- Long stick or yardstick

NUMBER *the flowerpots.*

A sundial has two main parts: the *plane* and the *gnomon (NOH mon)*. The plane is similar to the face of a clock or a watch. It is divided into 12 hours.

Your sundial will mark each hour with a flowerpot. Using the numbers 1 to 12, paint one number on each flowerpot. (The pot labeled 1 will represent one o'clock. The pot labeled 2 will represent two o'clock, and so on.) When you finish, you should have one plain flowerpot left.

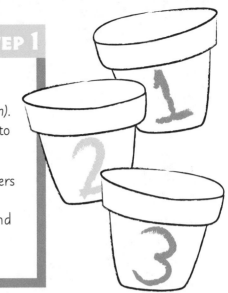

DECORATE *the flowerpots.*

Time to get creative! Many old sundials were decorated with the signs of the *zodiac*. The zodiac is a band of the sky that contains 12 star systems. Each system has its own special symbol.

You can also paint scenes from your life here on Earth. Think about the activities that are part of your daily life. (Meals, hobbies, and sports are good places to start.) Paint something that symbolizes each activity on the appropriate flowerpot. For example, if you usually wake up at 7 am, draw an alarm clock on flowerpot 7.

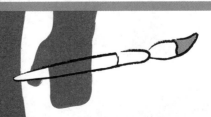

129

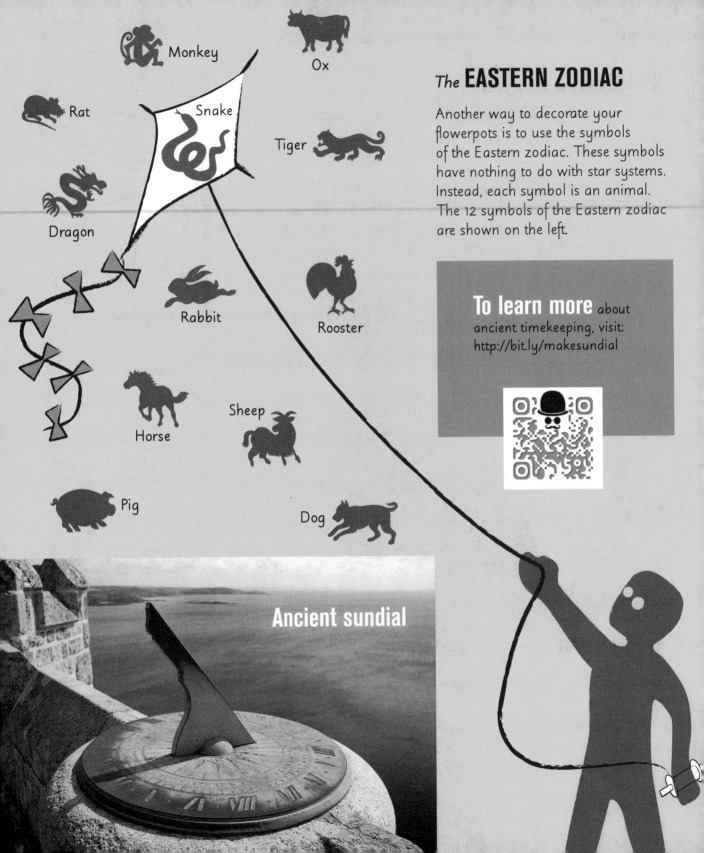

Monkey

Ox

Rat

Snake

Tiger

Dragon

Rabbit

Rooster

Horse

Sheep

Pig

Dog

The **EASTERN ZODIAC**

Another way to decorate your flowerpots is to use the symbols of the Eastern zodiac. These symbols have nothing to do with star systems. Instead, each symbol is an animal. The 12 symbols of the Eastern zodiac are shown on the left.

To learn more about ancient timekeeping, visit: http://bit.ly/makesundial

Ancient sundial

SET UP *the gnomon and the plane.*

The *gnomon* is similar to the hour hand on a clock. The shadow the gnomon casts tells you what time it is. To make your gnomon, fill the plain flowerpot with dirt. Poke a long stick deep into the dirt. It should stand up straight in the pot. Now, set up the plane by finding a flat patch of grass in a sunny area outside. (You don't want anything to block sunshine, such as trees and buildings.) Place the pot with your gnomon in the middle of this area.

The shadow that the gnomon casts throughout the day will tell you where to place the numbered flowerpots. At the top of each hour, observe where the stick casts its shadow. Place the corresponding flowerpot at the tip of the shadow. So, for example, at 8 am, place flowerpot 8 at the tip of the shadow. At 9 am, place flowerpot 9 at the tip of the shadow.

Repeat this process every hour until sundown. Don't worry if you need to skip a few hours to do something else—you can fill in the gaps another day.

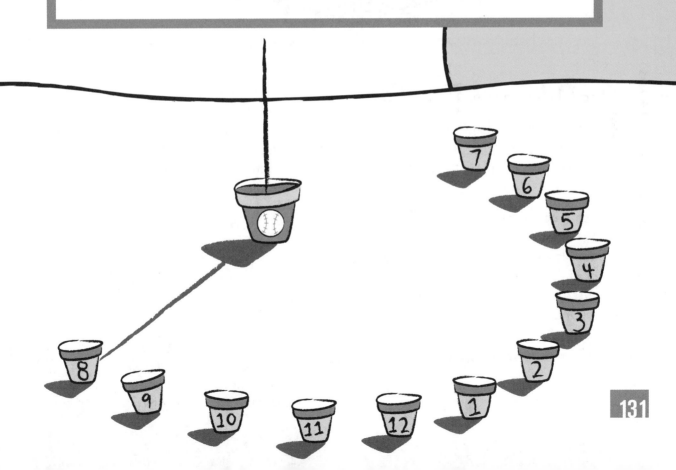

Read the shadows to **TELL TIME**.

As the sun moves across the sky from east to west, the shadow of your gnomon will move across the sundial. You should be able to tell the time by "reading" the position of the shadow. For example, if the shadow falls halfway between flowerpots 1 and 2, you'll know it's about 1:30 pm.

Each time you read your sundial, check your guess against your watch or another clock. Your guesses will get better with practice. Of course, the sundial only works during the day. Also, keep in mind that if you use it for more than a few weeks, you will need to adjust the flowerpots a little. The tilt of Earth causes regions of the world to receive different amounts of sunlight throughout the year.

Throughout the project, document the process with photography, video, drawing, graphing, writing, cartooning, music writing, or any other form.

The Sundial Bridge in Redding, California, is a modern-day sundial. The bridge is supported by a steel cable suspended from a 217-foot- (66-meter-) high post, which serves as a gnomon.

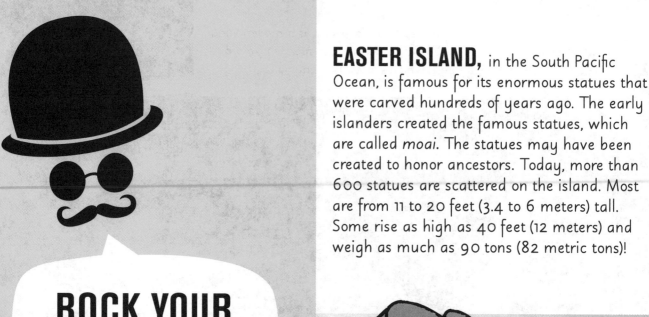

EASTER ISLAND, in the South Pacific Ocean, is famous for its enormous statues that were carved hundreds of years ago. The early islanders created the famous statues, which are called *moai*. The statues may have been created to honor ancestors. Today, more than 600 statues are scattered on the island. Most are from 11 to 20 feet (3.4 to 6 meters) tall. Some rise as high as 40 feet (12 meters) and weigh as much as 90 tons (82 metric tons)!

ROCK YOUR OWN STATUES

The islanders used stone hand picks to carve the statues from the rock of an extinct volcano. They set up the statues on raised temple platforms called *ahu*. Huge red stone cylinders were balanced on the heads of some of the statues, like hats. Even today, putting up such large statues and balancing the cylinders on top of them would be a difficult feat!

You can easily make your own miniature version of the stone statues of Easter Island. Just follow the steps in this activity!

MATERIALS:

- Lid from a shoe box (or other box), no higher than 2 to 3 inches (5 to 18 centimeters)
- Sand
- 3-5 oblong-shaped rocks, each about 5 inches to 6 inches (13 to 15 centimeters) tall
- Pencil
- Acrylic paint
- Small paint brushes
- Toothbrush
- School glue
- Moss
- White polymer clay or sculpting clay dough (see page 137 for instructions on how to make sculpting clay dough)
- Dried grass
- Old plate or plastic plate
- Old newspaper
- Seashells
- Old fork or plastic fork
- Camera, video camera, and/or writing materials

Scientists disagree about how early islanders moved the huge stone statues the 11-mile (18-kilometer) distance from the place where they were carved to the platforms where they sit today. Some scientists believe the statues were designed to rock back and forth in a vertical position. With this design, the islanders may have been able to move the statues using only ropes and human strength!

Give your rock **A FACE.**

You can paint your rocks to look like the Easter Island statues, or design your own fun faces.

Find the flattest side on each stone. Draw a face on it with a pencil. Use the old plate to mix paint colors. For a natural look, mix a paint color that is as close to the rock color as possible. Then add black, brown, or gray to paint the shaded parts of the face, such as under the eyebrows, the bottom of the nose, or the top lip. Mix white to make the highlighted parts of the face, such as the tip of the nose or the bottom lip. Or go wild with fun colors! Let the faces dry a bit before moving to the next step.

Let your rocks **GATHER SOME MOSS.**

Mix some bright green paint and splatter it on the rocks with the toothbrush to get a mossy effect. Or you can do the same with a little black paint or any of the natural colors you mixed before. Leave the rocks to dry.

MAKE A HAT *for your statue.*

Some of the moai statues at Easter Island wear red hats or topknots called *pukao*. The pukao were carved from volcanic stone. You can make pukao for your rocks using white polymer clay or sculpting clay dough (see the recipe below).

Mold the clay into a shape like the pukao shown on page 134 or make your own hat shape. Let the clay air dry.

After the clay is dry, paint the hat red to look like the pukao shown in the photo, or paint it any color you wish. Make hats for as many of the statues as you like.

Let the paint dry.

How to make SCULPTING CLAY DOUGH

MATERIALS:
- Saucepan
- 1 cup cornstarch
- 2 cups baking soda
- 1¼ cups water
- Waxed paper

In a saucepan, mix the cornstarch, baking soda, and water. With an adult's help, heat the mixture over a medium heat. Stir the mixture continuously until it thickens. Let it cool.

Place a sheet of waxed paper over your work surface. Knead the clay dough for a few minutes. Roll the clay into a ball and shape it. Let the clay air dry before painting.

If you want to play with the clay another day, store it in a sealed plastic bag or an airtight container and keep it in the refrigerator.

STEP 4

DECORATE *the box.*

You can display your statues inside the lid of the shoebox. But first, you need to decorate it! To start, sprinkle some dry grass, moss, and sand on the newspaper.

Cover the sides of the lid with glue. Roll the sides of the box in the mixture or sprinkle the mixture on the glued sides.

Throughout the project,
document the process with photography, video, drawing, graphing, writing, cartooning, music writing, or any other form.

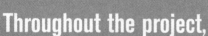

STEP 5

Fill the box with **SAND AND SHELLS.**

PLACE *the rocks in the sand.*

Sink the rocks a little into the sand to make them stand up.

You can stand the rocks in a row, facing the same way, or position some to face one another. Have fun and experiment!

You can reposition the rocks over and over again. Just rake the sand with a fork and then rearrange your statues.

To learn more about Easter Island, visit: http://bit.ly/rockstatues

139

MINOTAUR
MASK

ONE OF THE MOST TERRIFYING

monsters in Greek mythology is the Minotaur (*MIHN uh tawr*), which had the head of a bull and the body of a man. According to legend, the Minotaur lived in a giant maze called a *labyrinth*. Every year, the king sacrificed seven boys and seven girls by sending them into the Minotaur's den.

In this project, you'll transform yourself into a Minotaur. You already have a human body—now you just need to make a scary bull mask!

MATERIALS:

- Newspaper
- 2 cups flour
- 2 cups warm water
- 1 tablespoon salt
- Bowl
- Whisk
- Balloon
- Small bowl filled with water
- Pin or tack
- Thick black marker
- Tracing paper (2 sheets)
- Pen or pencil
- Thin cardboard (or recycled cereal box)
- Scissors
- Masking tape
- Retractable utility knife
- Acrylic paint
- Paintbrush

The Minotaur
appears in paintings, pottery,
and other works of art from
ancient Greece.

STEP 1

Get ready to **MAKE A MESS.**

You will use a technique called *papier-mâché*
to make your mask. Papier-mâché is messy,
so be sure to cover your work area with
newspaper. You'll need more newspaper to
tear into strips for the papier-mâché. The strips
should be about 1 inch (2.5 centimeters) wide
and 6 to 8 inches (15 to 20 centimeters) long.

A homemade paste will help you mold the
strips into a mask. Combine the flour, water,
and salt in a bowl. Whisk it until the mixture is
smooth. (No lumps!) Its consistency should be
similar to cream or pancake batter. If the paste
seems too thick, add extra water, 1 tablespoon
at a time. If it seems soupy, add more flour.

To learn more about the Minotaur,
visit: http://bit.ly/minotaurmask

STEP 2

MAKE THE BASE *of your mask.*

Blow up a balloon until it's about the same size as your head. Dip a newspaper strip in the paste. (Remove extra paste by running the strip between two fingers.) Cover the top of the balloon with strips. Then cover half of the long part of the balloon with more strips.

Make sure you add the strips one layer at a time. Each layer needs to dry for an hour or two before you add more strips. (You'll need four or five layers total.) When you're finished, leave your mask to dry overnight. Be patient! Your mask might break if you rush this step.

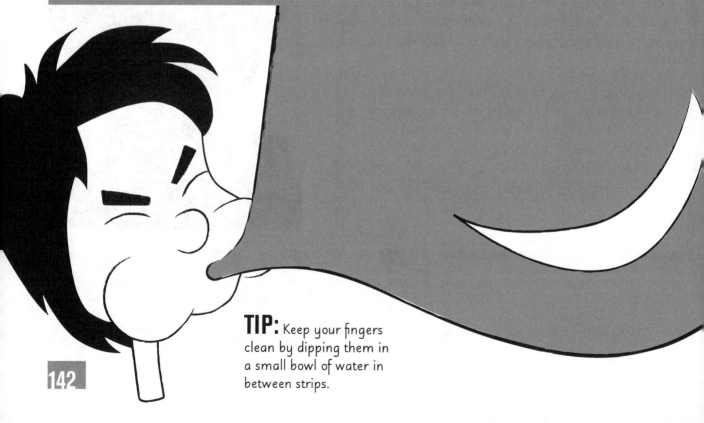

TIP: Keep your fingers clean by dipping them in a small bowl of water in between strips.

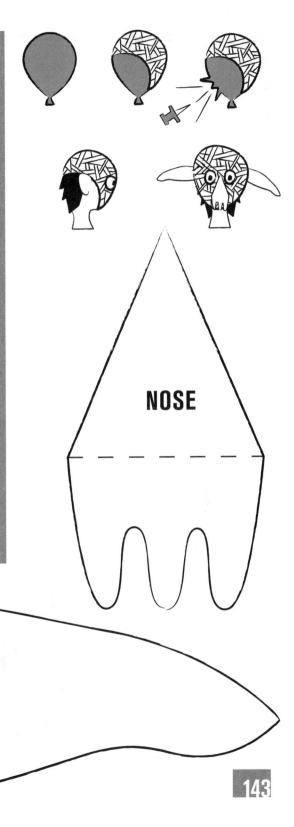

STEP 3

Start adding **FEATURES.**

Like you, a bull has two eyes, two ears, and a nose. To help your Minotaur see and breathe, you'll need to cut two eyeholes and two nostrils. First, use a pin to pop the balloon. (You can discard the balloon.) Try on the mask with the long side covering your face. Ask an adult to mark where your eyes and nostrils are with a black marker. Remove the mask. Have an adult cut two large openings for your eyes and nostrils using a retractable utility knife.

You'll use a template to help make the nose and ears. (Note: these features are just for decoration.) Begin by placing a sheet of tracing paper over the ear template. Trace two pieces carefully with a pen. Tape the tracing paper on a piece of cardboard. Use scissors to cut out the pieces. Discard the tracing paper.

Now repeat the tracing process with the nose template. When you've cut the nose piece from the cardboard, fold it along the dotted line. Now tape the nose and the ears into place with masking tape. Check the diagram as you go to make sure you're on the right track.

NOSE

EAR

MAKE *the horns.*

Bull horns are large and hollow. To start making your horns, roll up a whole sheet of newspaper into the shape of a horn. (Start rolling from the short end.) Twist the newspaper until you're happy with its shape. Make sure one end is pointy. When you're finished, wrap the horn in masking tape so it holds its shape. Now repeat the process for a second horn.

Tape the wide ends of the horns to the top of the mask. Use more strips of papier-mâché to cover the horns, the nose, and the ears. (You may need to make a second batch of paste.) Cover the taped areas with extra newspaper strips to reinforce the connections. Leave the mask to dry for at least 2 hours, or until it's completely dry.

STEP 5

Paint YOUR MASK.

Think about how you want to decorate your mask. Do you want it to look like a real bull? If so, keep in mind that a bull's hair is usually black, white, or red. Use one or more of these colors for a natural look.

Then again, maybe you don't want your mask to look realistic. (A Minotaur is a mythological creature, after all!) Feel free to be as creative as you like, but make sure you give your mask a mouth and eyebrows. Finally, remember to let the paint dry before you move the mask.

Throughout the project,

document the process with photography, video, drawing, graphing, writing, cartooning, music writing, or any other form.

MAKE YOUR OWN BACKGAMMON BOARD – Travel Edition

BACKGAMMON is a two-person game played with a rectangular board, playing pieces called *checkers* (or *men*), and dice. It's one of the oldest known board games, dating back to about 3000 B.C. Backgammon has been popular for so long because it's easy to learn and play, but it also requires strategy.

In this activity, you'll make a travel version of a backgammon board so you can bring the game with you wherever you go.

MATERIALS:

- 3-4 pieces of fabric material, each about 16 inches (40 centimeters) square. (Material that does not fray, such as felt, works best. Each piece of fabric should be a different color, but it doesn't matter if it's a solid color or a pattern.)
- Scissors
- Fabric glue
- Ruler
- 2 dice
- 15 blue buttons and 15 white buttons, each about 1 inch (2.5 centimeters) in diameter (Note: you can choose different colors, as long as you have 15 buttons of each color.)
- Cardboard tube about 12 inches (30 centimeters) long, such as a paper towel roll, or a similar tube-shaped canister
- Rubber bands
- Markers (optional)

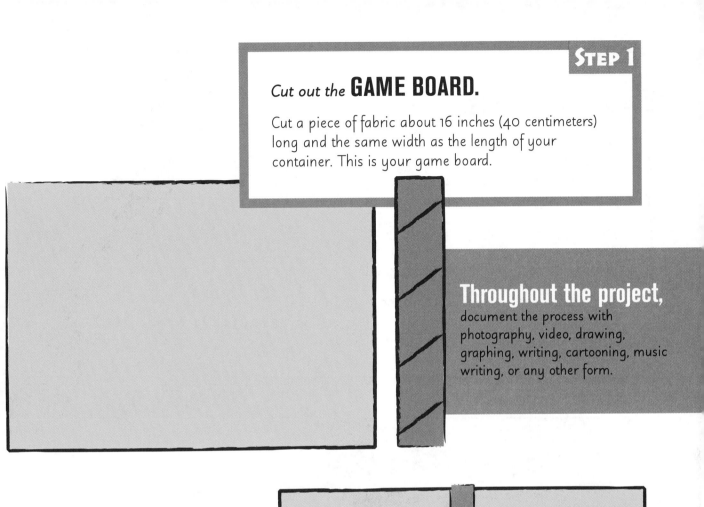

Cut out the **GAME BOARD.**

Cut a piece of fabric about 16 inches (40 centimeters) long and the same width as the length of your container. This is your game board.

Throughout the project, document the process with photography, video, drawing, graphing, writing, cartooning, music writing, or any other form.

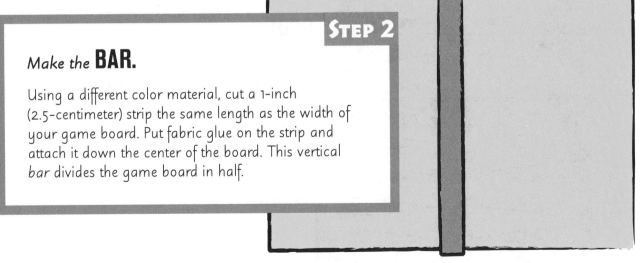

STEP 2

Make the **BAR.**

Using a different color material, cut a 1-inch (2.5-centimeter) strip the same length as the width of your game board. Put fabric glue on the strip and attach it down the center of the board. This vertical *bar* divides the game board in half.

Make **THE POINTS.**

Use a material that's a different color than the game board to make 24 *points*, the triangle-shaped divisions that line each side of the game board. If you have several different colors of fabric, you can alternate the colors of your points. Be creative!

Cut your fabric into 24 strips, each 1 inch (2.5 centimeters) wide by 5 inches (13 centimeters) long. Fold each strip in half lengthwise and draw a diagonal line from one corner to the opposite far corner.

Keeping the fabric folded, cut along the diagonal line. Open the fold to reveal the point. (Note: For each point, you'll have two leftover scraps that you can use later to decorate your travel container.)

GLUE *the points.*

Use the fabric glue to attach the 24 points along both long sides of the game board, pointing toward the center. There should be 12 points on each long side, with 6 on either side of the bar. Now your game board is complete!

STEP 5

Gather the dice and CHECKERS.

Gather 2 dice and 30 buttons (15 blue, 15 white). The buttons are your checkers, or playing pieces.

Now you have everything you need to play backgammon! Have fun!

Backgammon has been popular for more than 5,000 years. This illustration of two men enjoying the game dates from the late 1200's. It appeared in a book about board games.

For instructions on how to play backgammon, visit:
http://bit.ly/backgamboard

TRAVEL CONTAINER

(For open-ended tubes, follow all the steps. If you have a canister with a lid, skip ahead to Step 4.)

(For open-ended tubes, follow all the steps. If you have a canister with a lid, skip ahead to Step 4.)

CUT OUT *the fabric.*

Cut a piece of fabric a bit longer than the length of your tube, so that there is enough extra material to cover both of the open ends. The fabric should be wide enough to wrap around your container.

Seal one end of the **TUBE.**

Use the fabric glue to seal some extra material over one end of the tube. Next, cover the inside surface of the fabric with glue, and wrap it around the tube. Make sure the bottom end is completely sealed!

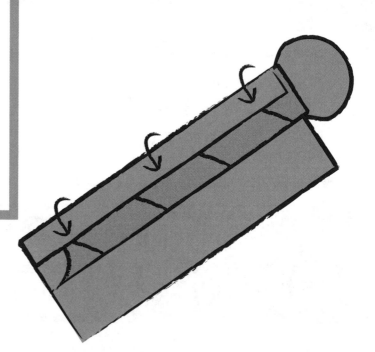

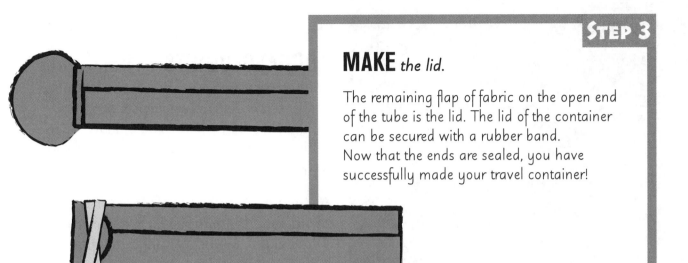

MAKE *the lid.*

The remaining flap of fabric on the open end of the tube is the lid. The lid of the container can be secured with a rubber band.
Now that the ends are sealed, you have successfully made your travel container!

STEP 4

DECORATE *your travel container.*

Use the leftover scraps of fabric and fabric glue to decorate your container. You can also draw designs with markers.

After you're finished playing, wrap your game board around the container and secure it with rubber bands. Store the dice and buttons inside of the container. You can also find backgammon game rules online, and print them so you always remember how to play. Put the rules inside of the container, too!

Now you're ready to play backgammon any place you travel!

ARCHAEOLOGICAL DIG

ARCHAEOLOGISTS are scientists who study the lives of people in the past. Unlike many scientists, archaeologists don't do all their work in white coats indoors. They gather most of their information by digging in the dirt.

As they dig, archaeologists look for clues about what life was like for our ancestors. Those clues can include anything, from tools, jewelry, and artwork to skeletons and the ruins of ancient buildings and other structures. All of these items tell archaeologists about the lives of people in the past.

In this activity, you'll create your very own archaeological site. Get ready to dig in!

MATERIALS:

- Newspaper
- Shoebox
- Artifacts (to bury): coins, leaves, buttons, flowers, apple core, gum wrappers, letters, etc.
- Plaster (enough to fill the shoebox)
- Sand or dirt
- 9 toothpicks
- String or dental floss
- Ruler
- Plastic gloves (optional)
- Digging tools: old toothbrush, tweezers, butter knife, spoon, small paintbrush, etc.
- Graph paper
- Camera (or art supplies) and writing materials

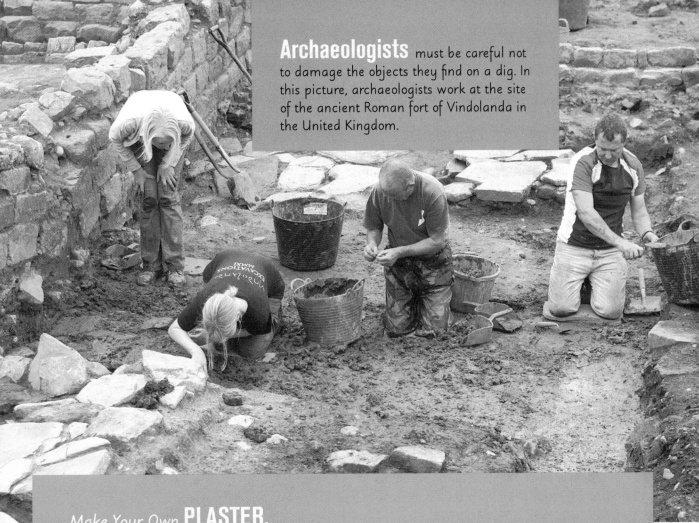

Archaeologists must be careful not to damage the objects they find on a dig. In this picture, archaeologists work at the site of the ancient Roman fort of Vindolanda in the United Kingdom.

Make Your Own PLASTER.

You can use sand or dirt to make a great dig. But if you really want to put your tools to work, plaster is the way to go. Plaster mix is sold at most craft stores. You can also make it at home with flour and water. This recipe makes a few cups of plaster. If you need more, simply double the recipe.

Combine 3 cups of flour and 1 cup of warm water in a large bowl. Stir the mixture with a wooden spoon for 1 minute. (Make sure it's smooth—no lumps!) Knead the dough with your hands for about 5 minutes. If the dough seems too thick, add more water 1 tablespoon at a time. If it seems too soupy, add more flour.

WARNING: Never pour the plaster down the sink because it can clog the pipes. Discard any leftover plaster in the trash or in a compost bin.

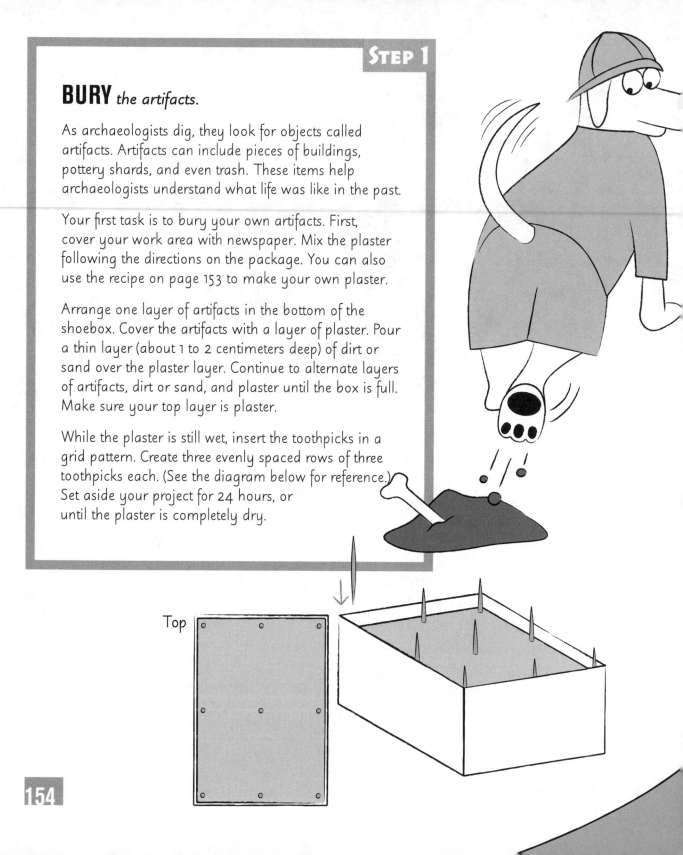

BURY *the artifacts.*

As archaeologists dig, they look for objects called artifacts. Artifacts can include pieces of buildings, pottery shards, and even trash. These items help archaeologists understand what life was like in the past.

Your first task is to bury your own artifacts. First, cover your work area with newspaper. Mix the plaster following the directions on the package. You can also use the recipe on page 153 to make your own plaster.

Arrange one layer of artifacts in the bottom of the shoebox. Cover the artifacts with a layer of plaster. Pour a thin layer (about 1 to 2 centimeters deep) of dirt or sand over the plaster layer. Continue to alternate layers of artifacts, dirt or sand, and plaster until the box is full. Make sure your top layer is plaster.

While the plaster is still wet, insert the toothpicks in a grid pattern. Create three evenly spaced rows of three toothpicks each. (See the diagram below for reference.) Set aside your project for 24 hours, or until the plaster is completely dry.

Top

Survey the SITE.

Archaeologists hunt for information before they begin digging. They keep detailed written records, photographs, maps, and plans of the dig site. Often, they start by dividing the surface into a grid. They take detailed notes and draw a map of the grid. Finally, they examine the squares of the grid one by one.

To start your survey, cover your work area with newspaper and peel away the shoebox from the plaster. Tie a long piece of string around one of the toothpicks. Run the string between the toothpicks to create four sections of the grid. Finally, use graph paper to draw a map of your grid. Take detailed notes about how it looks. Make sure to note any breaks or cracks in the plaster.

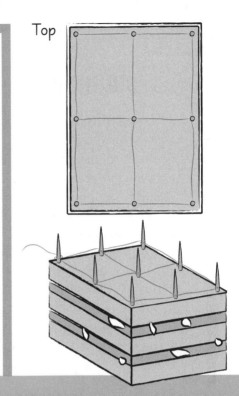

Top

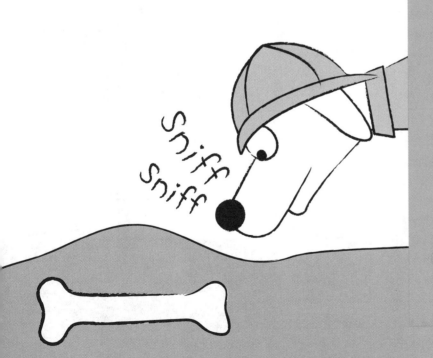

Sniff
Sniff

Learning the Lingo

Technically speaking, an "artifact" is an object made by human hands. An "ecofact" is a natural object, like the seed of an apple. Archaeologists look for both artifacts and ecofacts as they dig.

The chart below shows several examples of artifacts and ecofacts. Make a list of the objects you buried. Be sure you put each one in the right category!

Artifacts	Ecofacts
Coin	Apple seed
Toy	Chicken bone
Button	Leaf

Start DIGGING!

Archaeologists dig for artifacts in a process called *excavation*. They must be very careful not to harm the artifacts. Their exact method of excavation depends on the place where they're digging. They might use different tools to work inside a cave than they would use in an open field. As they work, they record the locations of where artifacts are found on a map of the grid.

To help protect your artifacts, put on your plastic gloves, if you're using them. Start with the largest tools to chip away the plaster. Dig within one section of the grid at a time. Work slowly and carefully.

Switch to smaller tools as you get closer to the buried objects. Try to remove as much of the plaster as possible without damaging the objects. Record your observations as you work. Make sure you show where you found each artifact on your map and how deep it was from the top.

To learn more about archaeology, visit: http://bit.ly/archaedig

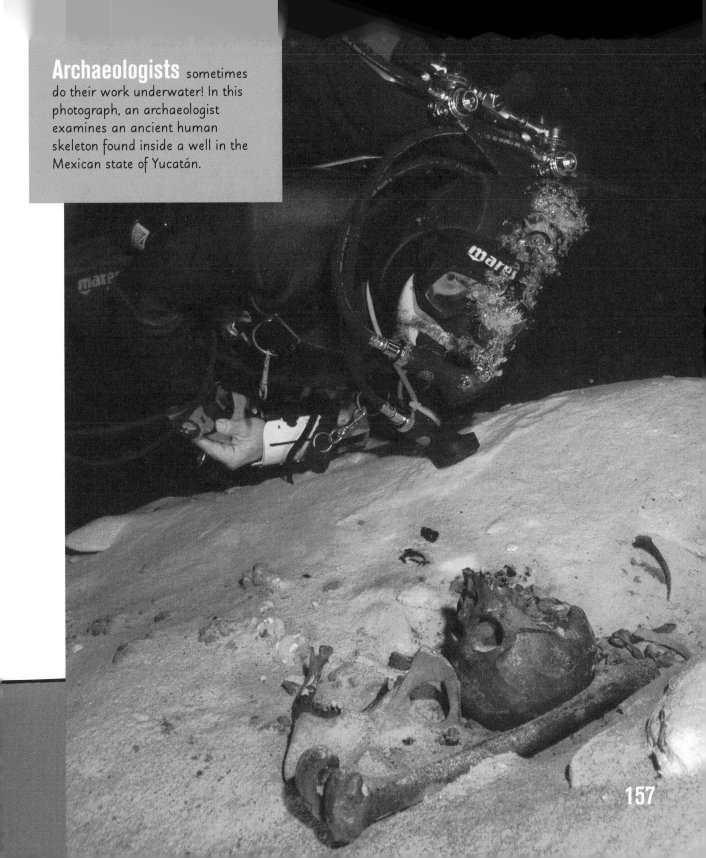

Archaeologists sometimes do their work underwater! In this photograph, an archaeologist examines an ancient human skeleton found inside a well in the Mexican state of Yucatán.

INTERPRET *your findings.*

Archaeologists spend a lot of time studying the objects they find. They group artifacts according to type and by location. Dating is an important step in this process. Archaeologists want to know how old items are. Sometimes they can determine an exact date. Other times they have to guess.

When you have uncovered all your artifacts, group the items. You might group them by type, size, color, or some other category. Next, try to determine the age of each object. (If you're not sure, make an educated guess.) Objects found in lower layers are likely older than items found in upper layers. Gather as much information as you can about each artifact. Record your findings as you go.

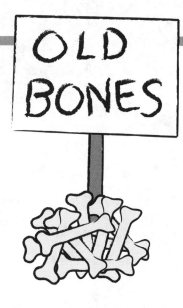

Throughout the project, document the process with photography, video, drawing, graphing, writing, cartooning, music writing, or any other form.

A helmet, a pitcher, and tools are some of the many objects archaeologists found in a well at Jamestown, the first permanent English settlement in the New World. The objects, now in a museum display, are arranged according to the depth at which they were found. Jamestown was founded in 1607 in present-day Virginia.